PREACHING ON SUFFERING AND A GOD OF LOVE

Henry J. Young
editor

with a Foreword by
Nathan A. Scott, Jr.

and contributions by

George Thomas

Robert Avon Bennett

Quinland R. Gordon

Howard W. Creecy, Sr.

Obie Wright, Jr.

Cecil Wayne Cone

Mance C. Jackson

John R. Bryant

Thomas Hoyt, Jr.

Charles Shelby Rooks

Gardner C. Taylor

Donald R. Wheelock

Edward P. Wimberly

FORTRESS PRESS   **Philadelphia**

Biblical quotations from the Revised Standard Version of the
Bible, copyright 1946, 1952, © 1971, 1973 by the Division of
Christian Education of the National Council of the Churches of
Christ in the U.S.A., are used by permission.
Biblical quotations from Today's English Version of the New
Testament, copyright © 1966 by American Bible Society, are
used by permission.

COPYRIGHT © 1978 BY FORTRESS PRESS

Library of Congress Cataloging in Publication Data

Main entry under title:
Preaching on Suffering and a God of Love.

Includes bibliographical references.
CONTENTS: Old Testament themes: Thomas G.
Transforming the tragic into the creative.
Bennett, R. A. Joseph: can good come out of evil?
Gordon, Q. R. The rescuing love of God. Creecy,
Sr., H. W. Aunt Hagar and her children. Wright,
Jr., O. They that wait for the Lord. [etc.]
    1. Suffering--Sermons.   2. Sermons,
American--Afro-American authors.   I.   Young,
Henry J., 1943—   II. Thomas, George
BV4909.P73   242'.4   77-15250
ISBN 0-8006-1332-5

6507A78   Printed in the United States of America   1–1332

To my parents,
Mr. and Mrs. Marion Young

CONTENTS

FOREWORD:
THE BURDENS AND TEMPTATIONS
OF THE PULPIT

Of all the myriad issues of life which the Christian pulpit is required to handle there is none so pressing, so inescapable, and so burdensome for the preacher as the problem of suffering, the mystery of iniquity, the strange and brutal haphazardness with which, as it seems at times, acute misfortune is distributed amongst men. The parson—who in his common aspect is not normally one endowed with exceptional gifts of intelligence and sensibility—suddenly finds himself having to preside over the last rites for a little girl who had been wonderfully beautiful and vivacious and who, her parents' only child, was fatally stricken with cerebral meningitis. Or—as in that sad case of the early sixties in Holcomb, Kansas, that occasioned Truman Capote's brilliant book *In Cold Blood* (1965)—an entire family, say, is fiendishly murdered by some beast of prey, a family loved and respected by all who had known them; and their pastor has finally to stand over their coffins and try to help their grieving friends and neighbors to assimilate the event, to situate in their universe of meanings an assault against life to which no decent meaning can easily be assigned. Or, again, a whole town may be visited with disaster by tornado or flood, and, on the Sunday afterward, whoever it is who occupies a pulpit will find himself facing people suddenly bereft of relatives and friends and homes, and asking that overwhelming question that Lear voices amidst the thunder and pelting rain of his lonely heath: "Is man no more than this?"

Here it is, indeed, on such occasions as these, that those entrusted with the proclamation of the gospel find themselves well-nigh overborne by what is perhaps the most daunting burden of the Christian pulpit, of accommodating the doctrine of Providence to the slings and arrows of outrageous fortune. For that doctrine says, of course, that the world is basically *for* us rather than *against* us and that no ache or wound or woe is beyond God's power to heal and save: it denies, in other words, that absurdity is the reigning principle of human existence. And it may even be the case that those representing any sort of resolute commitment to the primitive radicalism of the Christian faith find it far more difficult than others do to absorb the tragic things of life, since their expectation that good shall prevail leaves them peculiarly vulnerable to the shock called forth when they are overtaken by what appears to be some fundamental breakdown or wreckage of life.

Now, in undertaking to reckon with this most awesome burden of the pulpit, as he must regularly do and often on occasions of enormous stress, the special temptation that the preacher needs greatly to resist is that of being in so great a hurry to resolve enigma as to claim to know more than he really does about what Lear calls "the mystery of things." And on this matter the late Albert Camus offers a fine cautionary parable in his novel of 1947, *La Peste* (The Plague). The setting of the action is the Algerian coast town of Oran, whose inhabitants begin to notice one spring in the early 1940s that their residences are increasingly overrun with rats. Indeed, after a day or so rats are tumbling out of basements and sewers in vast droves, all over the town, and, increasingly, the local radio news broadcasts begin to be largely given over to bulletins about just how many thousands of rats were collected and burned within a span of so many hours. As the days go by, the situation steadily worsens: more and more dead vermin are filling the streets, their "shrill little death-cries" being heard everywhere at night and the truckloads of mice being collected by the municipal sanitation department growing ever larger. So that which had at first been merely a strange and unprecedented nuisance to be grumbled about comes at last to seem a phenomenon vaguely portentous and menacing.

Then the townspeople begin to die of a strange fever, and the local physicians very shortly realize that all the circumstances require the conclusion that Oran has been stricken by bubonic plague. So, with the closing of the city gates, the entire population is placed under quarantine, and, for what proves to be the better part of a year, the people are closed off from the rest of the world and shut in upon a long ordeal of suffering and death.

Camus selected as the epigraph for the novel a sentence of Daniel Defoe's which says, "It is as reasonable to represent one kind of imprisonment by another, as it is to represent anything that really exists by that which exists not." And thus he was at pains to underscore what is manifestly an allegorical purpose, for the plague is, of course, but an emblem of all the shocks that flesh is heir to, of everything that humiliates and harrows and wounds the human spirit in its voyage through the world. Moreover, much of what is most interesting in the novel is conveyed by the account it gives through its dramatis personae of the various responses that are made by the people of Oran to this great emergency. Some meet it with a quiet kind of courage and determination to be helpful to their neighbors. In some it calls forth heroism; in others it becomes an occasion for revealing cowardice. Some even seize it as an opportunity for contriving "black-market" operations of one sort or another and for profiteering on human suffering. And a variety of other responses to the crisis is represented by Camus' cast of characters.

It is, however, the priest, Father Paneloux, who deserves on this present occasion to be singled out, since his role in the novel makes him type and example of the special kind of mistake too frequently made by the clerical imagination in its response to the woes of the world. After the plague has been under way for several weeks and the ever mounting tallies of death refute all hope of its early abatement, the clergymen of the town organize a Week of Prayer which culminates in a great Mass in the local cathedral, and on this occasion Father Paneloux is asked by his fellow clergy to deliver the sermon. He is a man "of a passionate, fiery temperament" and one adept in all the arts of pulpit eloquence who,

once he has accepted the assignment, flings himself wholehearted-
ly into the necessary preparations. And on the appointed Sunday,
as he leans over the edge of the pulpit to peer down at the huge
congregation, he launches into his discourse in a calmly emphatic
tone by saying, "Calamity has come on you, my brethren, and, my
brethren, you deserve it . . . [Remember that] from the dawn of
recorded history the scourge of God has humbled the proud of
heart and laid low those who hardened themselves against Him.
Ponder this well, my friends, and fall on your knees." Indeed, the
whole sermon is "like a fisticuff":

> Yes, the hour has come for serious thought. You fondly imagined
> it was enough to visit God on Sundays, and thus you could make free
> of your weekdays. You believed some brief formalities, some bend-
> ings of the knee, would recompense Him well enough for your crim-
> inal indifference. But God is not mocked. These brief encounters
> could not sate the fierce hunger of His love. He wished to see you
> longer and more often; that is His manner of loving and, indeed, it is
> the only manner of loving. And this is why, wearied of waiting for you
> to come to Him, He loosed on you this visitation; and He has visited
> all the cities that offended against Him since the dawn of history.
> Now you are learning your lesson, the lesson that was learned by
> Cain and his offspring, by the people of Sodom and Gomorrah, by
> Job and Pharaoh, by all that hardened their hearts against Him. And
> like them you have been beholding mankind and all creation with
> new eyes, since the gates of this city closed on you and on the
> pestilence. Now, at last, you know the hour has struck to bend your
> thoughts to first and last things.

In short, Father Paneloux chooses to pursue the high Deuter-
onomic line, that suffering is nothing other than a manifestation of
God's intention to reward sin with scourging and chastisement.
And the novel's narrator says that, having awakened in many of the
people of Oran a sense of being "sentenced . . . to an indeterminate
period of punishment" and of "undergoing a sort of incarceration,"
this "Sunday of the sermon marked the beginning of something like
a widespread panic in the town."

The world of the townsfolk has been invaded by the Absurd, but
Father Paneloux, by reason of his radical commitment to a traditional supernaturalist faith, dwells in a realm outside the Ab-

surd—and thus he intends unequivocally to proclaim, even in a time of trouble and despair, the absolute sovereignty of God. But though one may feel it regrettable that the stiff punctiliousness of his theological position cripples his capacity to offer comfort and hope to a stricken people, it is not so much this that forfeits our sympathies for him—but, rather, it is his overweening confidence in what is after all merely a formulaic resolution of the mystery of gratuitous suffering. And he prompts the same kind of recoil that was provoked in many of us by Heinrich Grüber, the distinguished dean of the Evangelical Church of East and West Berlin, who, though he risked his own life in the early forties in his efforts to smuggle Jews out of Germany, yet persisted long after the end of the Second World War in his contention that the hand of God was at work in the Holocaust toward the end of chastening his chosen people: *"Um deinetwillen werden wir getotet den ganzen Tag"* (for thy sake are we slaughtered every day).[1] But to this the riposte that many will hear echoing in their own hearts is that of Dostoevski's Ivan Karamazov—the high, silvery laughter of Ivan's "disgusted repudiation."

Now the great mistake, of course, that is made by the pulpit when it risks any sort of rational account of evil is that of permitting itself a view of things *sub specie aeternitatis.* For this is precisely where the preacher never stands, under the aspect of eternity: his view of the world, like that of everybody else, is always *sub specie temporalitatis.* And thus what is perhaps always the wisest course for him is that of carefully forswearing any and all attempts at explaining why tribulation and suffering overtake us, or how they are ultimately to be fitted into the total economy of an "engodded" world. For the gospel is found to be good news not because it explains how we come to be in what popular existentialism used to call "the human predicament" but rather because it proves itself to be an effective way of practically coping with that predicament. So a great reticence needs to be practiced about the issues of "cosmology," about how the fact of evil requires to be reconciled with a faith in the sovereignty over the world of a gracious and providential Presence. None of us knows how this is to be done, as the tangled contradictions in the history of Christian theodicy surely prove. And Christian preaching will doubtless be most authentic and helpful when it avoids any sort of speculative venture. The working pastor will, of course, over and again find himself facing people utterly ravaged by the question as to *why*, as to why the gospel should be offered any credence when it seems to be so absolutely contradicted by the facts of human experience. That remarkable Jewish philosopher, Emil Fackenheim, who intends not to forget the enormities of the Holocaust, asks, "At Auschwitz, did the grave win the victory after all, or, worse than the grave, did the Devil himself win?" But who can say? All that we can answer, as Dr. Fackenheim himself is wise enough to know, is that we must not now cooperate with Hitler in *his* grave, that we must not "despair of man and his world, and . . . escape into either cynicism or other-worldliness," that we must not hand over the world to "the forces of Auschwitz."[2]

And so, indeed, the question to which the Christian pulpit is best advised to dedicate itself is not the matter of *why* we are so badly abused, as at times we seem to be. Certainly it is a mistake for the issue ever to be so posed as to require the preacher to explain why it is that God "allows" a fatal automobile accident or a tornado or a cancer beyond surgical remedy, for, as Bishop Robinson reminds us, there is no intentionality of any sort at all in these things:

> The concatenation of events that produces earthquakes and accidents, the cruelties of natural selection and the indiscriminate sufferings of war, are not to be seen in terms of prevenient intention. . . . Taking the immanence, the incarnation, of God seriously as the form or field of his transcendence . . . means that categories of intentionality and the like are relevant only when the Divine is operating through personality. In the dense world of sub-personal relationship (which includes all but the self-conscious tip of human life, as well as the rest of nature), the purposiveness of love works itself out through "blinder" categories. There is no *intention* in an earthquake or an accident. But in and through it it is still possible to respond to the *Thou* that claims even this for meaning and personal purpose.[3]

Which suggests, then, that the great issue for the pulpit is not *why* we are assaulted by the various misfortunes that overtake us but how they "can be taken up and transformed rather than allowed to build up into a dark patch of loveless resentment and meaningless futility."⁴

The preacher's task, in other words, concerns not any sort of speculative or theoretical issue but the preeminently practical issue of how healing and redemptive meanings can be wrested from the experience, involving whatever degree of hardship, that life brings our way. And never does he stand *sub specie aeternitatis,* but always *sub specie temporalitatis*—there where the immediate question demanding to be addressed concerns how we may go about (as Paul phrases it) "redeeming the time" (Col. 4:5). But though his task is something more modest than Camus's Father Paneloux supposes, it is yet one sufficiently difficult to make it important that he constantly seek as much guidance as he can come by; and thus such a collection of sermons as this book presents is likely to be found by many working parsons "a very present help" indeed.

NATHAN A. SCOTT, JR.

Commonwealth Professor of Religious Studies
and Professor of English
The University of Virginia
Charlottesville, Virginia

NOTES

1. Dr. Grüber's citation is of Ps. 44:22. See Richard Rubenstein's account of his conversations with Dr. Grüber during the summer of 1961 in *After Auschwitz* (Indianapolis: Bobbs-Merrill Co., 1966), pp. 48-53.
2. Emil Fackenheim, *God's Presence in History* (New York: New York University Press, 1970), pp. 75, 84.
3. John A. T. Robinson, *Exploration into God* (Stanford, Calif.: Stanford University Press, 1967), pp. 117-118.
4. Ibid., p. 118.

PREFACE

Theodicy has been a central issue of the Christian faith through its entire history. The term comes from two Greek words meaning "God" and "justice"; it refers to the attempt to defend and justify the intrinsic goodness, mercy, righteousness, and love of God in face of the manifold presence of suffering in the world. The omnipotence of God is also a critical aspect of theodicy and can best be understood in light of a dilemma: Why does God permit human suffering to exist in the world? If he is able to eliminate human suffering and chooses not to, does this mean that he is not all-good and merciful? If he is unable to eliminate human suffering in the world, does this mean that he is not all-powerful? How do we resolve this dilemma of theodicy? Do we conclude that God is partial and favors certain groups? Do we conclude that history represents the eschatological unfolding of God's will, an activity beyond man's comprehension? Or do we conclude that God is responsible for human suffering? These questions have been the subject of academic debate for centuries.

The attempt of this volume is not to offer definitive answers to these questions. There aren't any answers. But there are viable ways of speaking meaningfully about God in spite of the dilemma of theodicy. Through various styles of black preaching, this volume suggests some of the ways black Americans have maintained integrity with God and themselves in spite of the continued presence of suffering, oppression, racism, poverty, violence, sickness, death, man's inhumanity to man, and other forms of social malfunctions. It shows how black Americans maintain a profound optimism, a growing edge of hope and a determination to look toward the eschatological future for freedom and liberation both within history and beyond history, rather than to succumb to pessimism, meaninglessness, hopelessness, despair, defeatism, atheism, agnosticism, and purposelessness.

The contradiction between God's intrinsic goodness and human suffering is neither ultimate nor final. It will eventually exhaust itself, making the ultimate destiny of humankind optimistic, triumphant, and good. Human suffering therefore, is transitory and episodic. God is a nontransitory reality that includes the vicissitudes and episodic transitories of existence in his nature, both sustaining and offering humankind a way of overcoming and rising above human suffering. This captures the taproot of black religion and demonstrates how black Americans have been able to survive the cruelties of slavery and man's inhumanity to man.

I want to express my deep appreciation to Nathan A. Scott, Jr. and to all the other contributors for their interest and cooperation at every stage of this project. I am also grateful to my secretary, Mrs. Gloria J. Herod, for typing the original manuscript, and to Mrs. Alma J. Bailey for help in copy editing.

HENRY J. YOUNG

PART ONE

OLD TESTAMENT THEMES

TRANSFORMING THE TRAGIC INTO THE CREATIVE

GEORGE THOMAS

Minister of Outreach and Institutional Relations
The Riverside Church
New York, New York

And the Lord God formed man of the dust of the ground, and breathed into his nostrils the breath of life; and man became a living soul.

—Genesis 2:7

The kingdom of God is within you.

—Luke 17:21

The Genesis creation story pictures God as creating human form out of the dust of the earth. God is then portrayed as breathing the breath of life into human form, making it a living soul. This means that God is the breath of life. I believe that the breath of God breathes in every living thing.

God is *in life,* not somewhere "up there." Paul Tillich talks about God in these words. He says, "God is the infinite, inexhaustible depth and ground of being." Rather than thinking of God as some being up there in the heavens, let us think of God as Ground, as Substance, as the Realty out of which all reality has come. Then you perceive that you find God by immersing yourself in the struggles and decisions of life. You find God in yourself and in others, and in history. God is not outside. God is "inside of reality breaking out."

God also integrates all of life. Howard Thurman uses an apt illustration: "If my little finger hurts so that it can no longer function like a little finger ought, then I become aware of it. I become 'little-finger conscious,' but when my finger is able to behave within the unity of the hand, then I say that my little finger is well, and by well I mean that it is restored to its natural place in the integration and coordination of the hand." That, to me, is the way life is. There is unity in the nature of existence. There is a relationship between me and the sun, between me and the earth, between me and the air, between me and the sea, between me and other persons. And if I am going to recognize and honor that interrelatedness, which God has woven into the fabric of life, then I must see to it that the air, the earth, the seas, and other human beings, have due justice and respect and the opportunity to breathe the breath of God.

No matter what we say about the nature of God, based upon the knowable world, based upon what existence reflects about the nature of God as we use our reasoning powers, there is still mystery—"For now we see through a glass darkly." Why cancer? Why children born blind? Why retardation? Why the crippling diseases that destroy the mind, the soul, and the body? A genuine faith resolves the mystery by ascertaining that at the center of reality, at the heart of the universe, there is meaning, not meaninglessness; love, not hostility. Life is not "a tale told by an idiot, full of sound and fury, signifying nothing"; life is full, a pregnant bursting forth in us of the purpose and energy and resources that abound throughout the totality of creation.

To discern God at work in the creative climate in nature and in human nature is not hard at all. But there is another climate in which it is more difficult to see God at work.

This climate is expressed by the words "*transforms death* (of spirit) *into life.*" This is the tragic climate. It is characteristically negative, disorderly, destructive, contradictory. It involves the tearing down of reality, whether it is the result of a terrible deed which one person does that affects another's life, or the subtle and massive injury of an institutional form, or the striking down of the innocent by natural causes which are a part of the intricacies and mysteries of the natural order. To believe that God can work within this setting is difficult indeed.

In the lives of all of us there are moments of building up and tearing down—the creative and the tragic. And the absolute prerequisite to live a full and healthful life is to have the internal capacity to cope, or better still, to transform the tragic experiences into creative encounters with life.

Let me share with you some of the ways I have experienced for accomplishing this.

First, recognize that because the breath of God breathes in you, the resources to transform the tragic into the creative are *in you.* Consider the tragic situation of Jesus and his people under military occupation by the powerful Roman Empire. Humiliation, depression, and degradation were the order of the day for the Jews in their own homeland. Their autonomy had been taken away. Taxes of all kinds were levied against them, and with this revenue temples were built to Emperor Augustus and Roman roads were laid—in part to make it easy for the Roman army to move with dispatch to put down any insurrection by the Jews.

Into this setting came Jesus and his words were directed to the House of Israel, who were embittered by the loss of their status as an empire of once far-reaching significance, and haunted by the vision of a new day. His message was a strategy for survival. It recognized that no power could ultimately destroy a people if it did not first win the victory of the spirit against them. Jesus said that the resource to transform their situation was in them, and Jesus called it the "kingdom of God."

As long as the breath of God breathes in you, there is something in you that is inviolate, that cannot be eradicated, obliterated, annihilated, or ultimately destroyed. It is a resource to equal any pain. It is an intrinsic value and worth. It is at once the breath of God and the kingdom of God.

Second, recognize that it is *your will* that holds the key to releasing the breath of God within you. For me to call upon God or to invoke the Spirit of God is *not* to cause God to do something God is *not* already doing. When I use the imperative mood and ask God to do this or that, it is more a recognition than a command. I am reminding myself of what is already going on and I am opening myself to the power flowing deeply within me.

It is the will that makes the difference. You may feel beaten by life. You may beat your chest and call yourself a failure. You may blame environment or society or a loveless childhood, or overprotective parents. But the crucial point in your life comes when you realize that you are not a prisoner of your past nor a victim of your wrongdoings. You can make a decision! You can change your life! And the Spirit within you will lift you!

Now we come to my last point: Recognize that we give life to each other. The breath of God breathes in all of us—we are members one of another. Do not deal with your tragedy alone. Remember that life comes to us from others in various ways, sometimes through a smile, or an encouraging word.

Just this week I received life through the beauty and grace and poetry of dance when I watched the Buffalo Black Dance Troupe here in the Riverside Theater, as it danced a religious and moving interpretation of life. It lifted me.

During Hitler's dictatorship Victor Frankl, a psychiatrist in Vienna, was placed in a concentration camp because of his Jewish ancestry. His father, mother, brother, and wife all died in the gas chambers. Only he and a sister survived. Later he wrote a book, *Man's Search for Meaning,* in which he told how he found the meaning of his life in the concentration camp. Let me paraphrase his discovery: "A human being is not one among other things. Things determine each other, but man is ultimately self-determining. What he becomes—within the limits of endowment and environment—he has made of himself." Let us pray:

> They that serve the Lord
>   shall renew their strength.
> They shall mount up with
>   wings as eagles.
> They shall run and not be weary.
> They shall walk and not faint. Amen.

JOSEPH: CAN GOOD COME OUT OF EVIL?

ROBERT AVON BENNETT

Associate Professor of Old Testament
Episcopal Theological School
Cambridge, Massachusetts

But Joseph said to them, "Fear not, for am I in the place of God? As for you, you meant evil against me; but God meant it for good, to bring it about that many people should be kept alive, as they are today. So do not fear; I will provide for you and your little ones."
—Genesis 50:19-21

The televised version of Alex Haley's book *Roots* has had a profound influence upon the American consciousness. The television dramatization, concentrated within the space of a week, had the impact of a massive dosage of some powerful medicine or drug. Some quarters, you will remember, feared that the portrayals of the brutal events of the slave trade and slave markets and the brutalization of blacks in American bondage would aggravate existing racial tensions and might even lead to violence. The *Roots* phenomenon seems, instead, to have triggered a quite unexpected development. The result of that shared experience by blacks and whites before their TVs on those evenings last winter was not a race war. Rather, blacks and whites began to take a deeper look at their respective heritages. Instead of coming out swinging at each other as some feared would happen after recalling the pain and guilt of slavery, the many ethnic as well as racial groups that make up America took up the task of tracing their roots. My wife's family had its first reunion ever, I am sure as a result of the impact of *Roots*. The press took note of the many ethnic groups which now began to look up their family trees. The *Roots* phenomenon has not brought us together, nor did it aggravate existing racial tensions, but it has

22

caused a whole people to take a closer look at their own particular backgrounds and family story.

We, as children of Africa and heirs of that shared horror called American chattel slavery, despite our love-hate relationship with America nevertheless find our roots in this land of our dispersion. Despite the pull of Africa as an ancestral home as shown in the many and continuing back-to-Africa schemes, the sentiment of the vast number of black Americans was and is already expressed by Frederick Douglass in his newspaper *North Star* (1849):

> Yet, if God wills that it (the Civil War) continue, until all the wealth piled up by the bondman's two hundred and fifty years of unrequited toil shall be sunk, and until every drop of blood drawn with the lash shall be paid with another drawn with the sword, as was said three thousand years ago, so still it must be said, "The judgments of the Lord are true and righteous altogether."

The ability of Martin Luther King, Jr. and the whole civil rights movement of the late 1950s and early 1960s to "prick the conscience of the nation" was based largely on this shared sense of injustice and the immorality of continued discrimination against the Negro.

While Alex Haley's work has got all of us thinking more about family trees and the stories contained therein, it singularly failed to place a theological interpretation upon the nightmare of slavery and American racism. Frederick Douglass and Martin Luther King, Jr. and even Abraham Lincoln, whose first priority was the saving of the Union, all saw God's hand lifted in judgment when brother persecuted brother simply because his skin color was different. The roots of black discontent lay in the brutalization and dehumanization caused by the denial of our God-given common humanity and natural kinship among peoples of the earth.

A phrase from an old spiritual best expresses the place of the Bible in shaping black faith in God's eternally good purposes for life:

> The Bible is our engineer
> That's what Satan's a-grumblin' about;
> It points the way to heav'n so clear,
> That's what Satan's a-grumblin' about.

The most significant part of our spiritual heritage, regrettably ignored in Haley's *Roots,* has been our unswerving trust in God's good intentions for black folk despite the evidence of the sorry history of bondage. An immediate bond was established between those who first heard the scriptural word in slavery and the Hebrew children's travail in Egypt portrayed in the Bible. Our story of sorrows is like their tales of woe, and the God who delivered them can and will deliver us. The sermons and the songs of black faith have rung the manifold changes on this good-news theme coming from the pages of the Bible.

The great preacher Howard Thurman noted some years ago that the similarity between black suffering and the biblical testimony helped forge the links between black faith and Scripture. Commenting on the words of the familiar spiritual,

> Were you there when they crucified my Lord?
> Were you there when they crucified my Lord?
> Oh! Sometimes it causes me to tremble, tremble, tremble,
> Were you there when they crucified my Lord?

Howard Thurman made a profound observation:

> The inference is that the singer was there; "I know what he went through because I have met him in the high places of pain, and I claim him as my brother." Here again the approach is not a conceptual one, but rather an experiential grasping of the quality of Jesus' experience, by virtue of the racial frustration of the singers.
>
> (Howard Thurman, *Deep River* [1955], p. 27)

The Old Testament story of Joseph sold into bondage by his brothers expresses more fully than any other the agony and the hope of black faith today. What is the meaning of the pain of continued racial oppression? How can we continue to trust in God's good intentions for humanity? Joseph in his agony of rejection and separation from his family faced a situation similar to that of the assaults on black trust in God's providential guidance. How could God let slavery happen in the first place, and why does he not intervene to end the racism which weighs us down to this very day?

The Bible opens with the story of the entire human family in the accounts of Adam and Eve, of Cain and Abel, of Noah and his sons, and of the builders of proud towers whose only achievement is to further confound the ability of people to understand one another and live together as the family God intended them to be. The focal point of Genesis is the call of Abraham and his children from among the families of the earth to serve as the instrument and guide for the nations to experience the power of God's blessing and grace: "And by you all the families of the earth shall bless themselves" (12:3).

Yet it was a hard and torturous road for Abraham and his wife Sarah to trust in God's promise to them. Even as Isaac the rightful heir was coming into his birthright, the slave woman, Hagar, and her son were being oppressed. Jacob sowed the seeds of enmity between himself and Esau, his brother, by cheating him out of his birthright. In each case, however, as with Abraham's willingness to sacrifice his son Isaac (chap. 22), and in Jacob's reconciliation with Esau (chaps. 32-33), these forefathers of God's elect people became changed people. Their experiences of faith transformed their lives, making them more fit to be the bearers of God's blessings to us all. Jacob's children, Joseph and his brothers, also had painful lessons to learn about their relationship to God and to one another. It is this story which black faith needs to hear again as we turn to God for reassurance.

No character or situation in the Bible is painted more vividly than that of Joseph. His older brothers were jealous of this young dreamer of dreams because of the favoritism shown Joseph by his father, and the younger son's tendency to lord it over his brothers. We recall Joseph's very special garment and the dreams which foretold his dominance over his older brothers. In a moment of anger they decided to rid themselves of this bothersome member and sold him off as a slave to foreigners who eventually brought him down into Egypt. The brothers attempted to cover up their heinous crime by telling a lie. They told Jacob that his son had been killed by a wild beast, and they even produced the fake evidence of Joseph's tattered and bloodstained robe. How cruel of the lads to so treat their own flesh and blood, to bring such sorrow to their father, and to bring such guilt upon their own consciences! It cannot be doubted that the lie they told to ease their consciences and to protect themselves from the wrath of Jacob was as great a burden to bear as was the foul deed itself.

The story of Joseph in Africa is well-known, from his troubles as a slave and his imprisonment to his meteoric rise at Pharaoh's court with the discovery of his special powers as an interpreter of dreams. These segments of his adventures in Africa, however, are not the main elements of this tale. Indeed, the black ancestors already grasped this truth, for their slave songs sang not of Joseph's wealth in Pharaoh's court, but of his betrayal by his brothers. The pain which opens our eyes to the meaning of this story comes out of the experience of the hatred and the lies told to cover up the hatred during slavery and afterwards. The truth coming out of the retelling of Joseph's story as it is heard among the oppressed and rejected is what must now be amplified and broadcast loud and clear. This is a story of betrayal, guilt, and fear, but also of forgiveness and reconciliation.

The reconciliation between oppressed and oppressor is described in the series of dramatic meetings between Joseph and his brothers in their moment of distress. It is to Joseph, now governor of Egypt's vast store of grain, that the brothers, now suffering the ravages of famine, must come for food. Famine in Canaan sends them to Africa where their brother had been sold a slave. Having taken on the customs, language, and dress of the land, Joseph is a stranger to them in their first interviews. Yet he recognizes them and devises a test to see if they have changed in their attitudes, not so much toward himself as toward their younger brother, Benjamin, and their aged father, Jacob. Were they still heartless and insensitive to the bonds of family so that they could reject a brother and lie to a father to cover up their crime? Joseph's test is a stern one. How would they react when their guilty consciences were pricked in being found guilty of crimes which they had not committed, and when forced to give up their younger brother Benjamin to win their release? Joseph demands that one brother be left behind as the others return to Canaan with grain, and further that when they come again they bring their youngest brother with them.

The harsh demands represent the first steps toward reconciliation. Joseph's test succeeds in that it forces the brothers to recognize and acknowledge their crime and guilt. The first part of this test makes them see that their present distress before this Egyptian is linked with their ill treatment of Joseph years before. Thinking he cannot understand them—an interpreter has been used for their negotiations for grain—they discuss their plight of having to leave one of their number as security in Joseph's presence. Even the stern Joseph must turn aside and weep as they unknowingly confess their sin before him.

The process of reunion between offended and offenders continues in the second interview when famine sends them to Joseph again, this time with Benjamin. The process of reconciliation continues with a still harsher demand that the beloved Benjamin must stay in Egypt. The plea in his behalf by the brother Judah shows that the men had indeed grown to respect one another and their father. Judah pleads for his brother and father and offers to stay on himself in place of the young lad. Rather than bring further sorrow to Jacob, Judah offers himself as substitute for the youngster's life. Moved by this profound demonstration of love and respect from the kinsmen who had so mistreated him, Joseph now reveals his true identity to the stunned brothers.

In making himself known to Judah, Benjamin, and the others, Joseph proclaims his conviction that it was God who had brought him to Africa and given him success there in order to preserve the life of his family. Three times in that second meeting when he revealed his identity, Joseph asserted, "God sent me before you to preserve life . . ." (45:5, 7-8). Only after he was convinced that his brothers were truly repentant did Joseph interpret their actions as part of God's divine plan of salvation. The modern saying that, "The devil might have brought you, but it was God who sent you," corresponds to the biblical proverb, "Many are the plans in the mind of a man, but it is the purpose of the Lord that will be established." (Prov. 19:21).

The patriarch Joseph could only show his brothers this new and profound faith in God's providential guidance once they could accept their guilt. Only after the harsh tests could they grasp the meaning of the words, "As for you, you meant evil against me; but God meant it for good . . ." (Gen. 50:20).

The goodness of God is revealed to us day by day. The changes which Joseph helped bring about in the evil attitudes of his kinsmen can take place in our world today. Yet each of us like Joseph must have faith in God's goodness and the willingness to stand stern tests of that faith. By the same token, we must also be ready like Joseph to confront our tormentors with the folly and evil of their ways. Reconciliation between oppressed and oppressor is no easy task. It requires strong faith and the vigilant demand for justice and changed attitudes among us all. Fundamental change in society as with radical transformation of one's life is no easy task. It is not achieved by superficial and facile means. This is not a simple "let's forgive and forget" proposition.

The horror of the cross and the agony of Jesus indicate the drastic means whereby God's good intentions overrule man's evil actions. It is our life in this Christ which permits us to hold Joseph's story as our story. With this affirmation of the change at work within our lives we can work as Joseph did to change the mind of our oppressors, even knowing it to be a long and arduous task. As we incorporate our lives more fully day by day into Christ's life, we can affirm with the Apostle, "We know that in everything God works for good with those who love him, who are called according to his purpose" (Rom. 8:28).

THE RESCUING LOVE OF GOD

QUINLAND R. GORDON

Dean of Absalom Jones Theological Institute
Atlanta, Georgia

On 5 January 1808 the Vestry of Saint Thomas African Episcopal Church met in session for a regular business meeting. One of the agenda items for that meeting was the following resolution that was presented for formal consideration, resolved: "That the thanks of the Vestry of Saint Thomas African Episcopal Church be presented to the Reverend Absalom Jones, Rector, for the sermon he preached in the said Church on the first day of January last, and that he be requested to furnish a copy of the same presented" (Extract from the Vestry Minutes, 5 January 1808, William Coleman, Secretary).

Following the unanimous adoption of this resolution, it was recorded in the Minutes of the Vestry for posterity. It referred to a sermon that Absalom Jones had preached to an overflowing congregation on 1 January 1808: "A Thanksgiving Sermon on Account of the Abolition of the African Slave Trade by the Congress of the United States." The Scripture text for his sermon was from Exodus 3:7-8: "And the Lord said, I have surely seen the affliction of my people which are in Egypt, and have heard their cry by reason of their taskmasters; for I know their sorrows; And I am come down to deliver them out of the hand of the Egyptians." In his sermon, Absalom Jones described some of the close parallels between the captivity of the children of Israel in Egypt and the captivity of the native Africans who were stolen from their tribal home in Africa and forced to accept a brutal existence as chattel slaves in the United

29

States of America. He said of the Israelites that they were deprived of their liberty, compelled to work in one of the hottest climates in the world without any covering from the rays of the sun. Their work was difficult and laborious and performed under the eyes of vigilant, rigorous masters, and the last deficiency in the product of their labor was punished by cruel lashes from the slave overseers.

I am sure that there are many people from all walks of life and nationalities who saw as I did—and notice I do not say enjoyed—the eight television chapters of the popular and acclaimed book *Roots* by Alex Haley. Those television shows reminded us once again that the cruel yoke of slavery forced upon our foreparents was a horrible nightmare that they had to endure each day. They too experienced the painful skin-cutting lashes from overseers, the grief and agony of separation from loved ones, and the constant heartbreaking denial of their freedom. When Absalom Jones preached his sermon to the people of Saint Thomas African Episcopal Church on 1 January 1808, he told them that the history of the world shows us with striking proof that the God who saw the affliction and heard the cries of the Israelites during their 400 years of oppressive servitude under the Egyptians was the same God who prevailed when the members of the Congress of the United States declared that the African slave trade would by act of law be stopped on 1 January 1808.

As I read and reread the sermon that was preached by Absalom Jones on that day of celebration 169 years ago, I was reminded constantly that the man who wrote and preached that sermon was born of slave parents in Sussex County, Delaware, on 6 November 1746. He experienced personally the binding shackles of slavery. At sixteen years of age he was separated from his mother, brother and sisters when they were sold to a new slave master, and he was taken to Philadelphia where he lived as a slave in bondage until 1784, when at the age of thirty-eight he was able to purchase his freedom. As I thought about Absalom Jones and his life experiences, I could not help but ask myself the question, I wonder if, during some of his dark and dismal days when his faith was weak and his hope overwhelmed by discouragement, Absalom Jones ever questioned the rescuing love of God, or pondered the questions: Where was God when the slave ships sailed from different ports in Europe and America, freighted with trinkets to be exchanged for the bodies and souls of men and women? Where was God when parents were torn from their children and children from their parents and placed in the dark and stinking dungeon of slave ships with their hands and feet bound in chains to be sold into slavery? Where was God when those chained bodies with souls made in his image were sold like horses and cattle upon the wharves of American seaports? Where was God when those slave-burdened bodies were driven into the sugar, rice and tobacco fields and compelled to work beneath a burning sun with scarcely enough clothing upon their bodies to protect them from the scorching rays?

I believe that if the former slave and priest of the church, Absalom Jones, could stand here with us today, his answers to those questions would be that as God was with his Christ and endured the agony and torture of that cross on Calvary's hill, that this same God was there in the miserable lives of those slaves of the past, and that he too was afflicted in their afflictions, that he suffered in their sufferings and shed with them the bitter tears of anguish as they endured the cruelty of man's inhumanity to his fellowman. Yes, I believe that Absalom Jones would say to us as he said to the people of his congregation on 1 January 1808, 169 years ago, that the rescuing love of God is the same yesterday, today and forever, that even during the harsh and seemingly godforsaken years of slavery, God was working his purpose out year by year. That God was working his purpose out in the lives of such prople as Sojourner Truth, who as a black woman, challenged the institution of slavery and worked diligently to eradicate this demonic evil from our society; that God was working his purpose out through Nathaniel Paul, militant antislavery advocate who encouraged the slaves to believe that slavery would be abolished because God willed it, and called upon them to oppose slavery with their hearts, minds, souls, and bodies. Yes, God was working his purpose out in the lives of such people as David Walker who wrote the "Appeal Against Slavery" in 1829 that became one of the most revolutionary documents to shake the foundations of the institution of slavery; that God was working his purpose out in the brief life span of Nat Turner who organized and executed the most unforgettable slave revolt in American history; that God was working his purpose out in the life of a man by the name of John Newton, a former captain of a slave ship, transporting slaves from the West Indies to England, but note how God worked his purpose out when John Newton was converted to Christianity and joined the Abolitionist movement in London as a militant spokesman against slavery. He was ordained a priest in the Anglican Church in 1764 and during his ministry, he became the author of such familiar hymns as "How Sweet the Name of Jesus Sounds in a Believer's Ears," "Glorious Things of Thee Are Spoken, Zion City of Our God," and "Amazing Grace! How Sweet the Sound That Saved a Wretch like Me."

Yes, God is always working his purpose out, not always as we would like, not always to accommodate our plans or to make life as comfortable for us or as free from trouble or pain or difficulty as we may pray for and want, but always, today and tomorrow and through the years, God is working his purpose out. I believe also that if Absalom Jones could stand here this morning as he stood before the congregation of Saint Thomas African Episcopal Church 169 years ago, he would say to us as he said to them, "Hold fast to the God of our forefathers." He would encourage us to remember that it was the religious faith and spiritual fortitude of our foreparents that kept them sane and humane and enabled them to survive the most brutal punishment inflicted on a people in the white western world.

As we recall the story of *Roots*, one of the major characters, Kunta Kinte, has given us an inspiring example that we should never forget. Even during his most dismal hours and hopeless days Kunta Kinte never forgot his Allah, his God, the God of his forefathers. He passed on this religious heritage to his children and his children's children and down through the years some remnants of this religious heritage have been passed on to us. May we never forget, forsake or deny that religious heritage, that life-sustaining spirit called the black religious experience that enabled our forefathers and foremothers to sing the songs of Zion in a barren, strange and unfriendly land. May we always remember the God of Kunta Kinte; the God of Absalom Jones; the God of David Walker, Sojourner Truth, Mary McCloud Bethune, Nat Turner, Frederick Douglass,

Daniel Alexander Payne, Henry Highland Garnet; the God James Weldon Johnson was talking about when he wrote the words:

> God of our weary years,
> God of our silent tears,
> Thou who hast brought us thus far on the way;
> Thou who hast by thy might
> Led us into the light,
> Keep us forever in the path, we pray.
> Lest our feet stray from the places, our God, where we met thee,
> Lest, our hearts drunk with the wine of the world, we forget thee;
> Shadowed beneath thy hand,
> May we forever stand,
> True to our God, true to our native land.

True to the God who delivered our foreparents from the blazing furnaces of slavery, true to the God who has said, "As I have overcome the world so will I help you to overcome." May this God have our highest allegiance, worship and servitude now and forever. Let us pray:

> Dear God, we thank thee for thy guiding and sustaining hand through the years. We thank thee for the life of Absalom Jones, born a slave 6 November 1746, died a revered priest of thy church, 13 February 1818. May we, like him, persevere to the end, in Jesus' name. Amen.

AUNT HAGAR AND HER CHILDREN

HOWARD W. CREECY, SR.

Minister of The Mount Moriah Baptist Church
Atlanta, Georgia

> Wherefore she [Sarah] said to Abraham, Cast out this bondwoman and her son: for the son of this bondwoman shall not be heir with my son, even with Isaac.
>
> —Genesis 21:10

In America we have a dual society. This dualism is sharply seen in the distinction between the haves and the have-nots, the whites and the nonwhites. It is as if there were two demons of destruction, racism and capitalism, and the two are rising for power.

Alienation and estrangement in human relationships has always been a problem. It is first a human problem; then it also becomes a divine problem. In the Bible (Gen. 16, 21, and 25) we find an interesting story of beginnings. It points out the basis for the beginning society and, after analysis, an understanding of this society. The American dream turns into a nightmare because of these two base problems, capitalism and racism.

We want to look at the black struggle in America in light of the biblical story of Hagar. We can see how Hagar and her children were able to survive in the contemporary culture by the power of God's presence in their lives.

Hagar was transported from her native land, Egypt, and uprooted from her heritage. She was brought into the household of Abraham as a slave. She was given the menial tasks to perform under the direction of Sarah, wife of Abraham and mistress of the house. She was subserviantly stripped of her womanhood as defined by that society.

Sarah had waited long years, wanting to be the instrumentality of God's promise by pregnancy. She interpreted her barrenness as hindering the promise of God to Abraham. God had promised that Abraham's descendants would outnumber the stars in the heavens and would match numbers with grains of sand on a seashore.

Sarah, as many others, sought to assist God out of his dilemma by offering her slave, Hagar, to Abraham to mate with before he was too old. The arrangements were made without Hagar's consent. She was called to be a substitute wife (chap. 16). Confusion in the texts relating to her status as a wife lead us to conclude that Hagar was sometimes regarded as wife. Mostly, she was just a part of a harem, or a night wife.

Hagar's body and mind were not a coordinated whole. She is now proud to be a chosen connecting link in God's continuance of creation and at the same time she is mentally depressed about her social position with a miscegenated child. Meanwhile, Sarah was having difficulty adjusting to the fact of Hagar's role in realizing the promise. Hagar was claiming too much attention from Abraham and became seemingly more important than Sarah. So the decision was reached that Hagar had to leave. Being used at such an emotional level, and then being asked to remember her position as a slave, dehumanized Hagar. She was physically afflicted by Sarah and forced out of the household as an uppity slave. She wandered to the south of Palestine, in the direction of Egypt (home), toward Beersheba. Now pregnant and disgusted, Hagar met God who dealt with her problem. God told her she would have a son who would lead a great nation. God promised to take care of her son and his descendants. Hagar returned to the household with assured security granted by God. She came back as a second-class citizen with strength to endure.

God granted Sarah in her old age the power of pregnancy. She bore a son according to the promise of God to Abraham and called him Isaac. When the two sons of Abraham were placed together at the weaning celebration of Isaac, Sarah accused Ishmael of mocking Isaac. Seemingly Hagar's son was at the point in life to challenge the system and thereby overturn the promise that Isaac would inherit the blessings of Abraham. In order to keep Ishmael in his place, second to Isaac, Sarah confronted Abraham about sending out the slave girl and her son.

Notice how in the biblical account the name of Hagar is dropped along with that of her son. They are known only as "girl" and "boy." In order to keep them subordinate they are stripped of their pride by lowering their estimate of themselves. This caused a restlessness in both of them. The man child, Ishmael, is known as a "wild ass" of a man—the term suggests his impatience with his segregated position in society. Abraham is sorry about the arrangement instigated by Sarah and talks with God who asures him that he will take the responsibility of rearing and caring for the mother and the child. Hagar goes south with meager rations and cares for her son. She had to do things without her male counterpart. In more modern times black men were forced from their families, and women by and large cared for the household. This created historically, in the black community, a matriarchal family. Hagar kept crying and caring while God took full responsibility.

God is still caring for his own. He is still making the impossible possible. The black family has been sustained amid the unwilling acceptance of moonlight social conditions with the hope of a sunlight tomorrow. That woman without a name has worked away from her home to make things better at home. With short hours at home she has inspired her man to soberly fight for freedom in spite of his temper of frustration and his feelings of fear. She has resisted and absorbed the resentment he has for those steering the system that disadvantaged him. She took the meager house and made it a home; no matter how humble, it was still home.

Hagar's children began at a great disadvantage. They started life in a wilderness, in a jungle of abuse. Their mother was called girl, or aunt, and they all are called boy and girl forever. They are forced to remember times when their mother was not with them and the undeserved whipping of society would cause their eyes to bleed tears. They are forced to remember the audible midnight crying of their mother from another room. All of Hagar's children will watch her weep in church and at home as she talks over her problems with God about her children. She seeks the God who met her one morning when her heart was heavy laden and she had a bowed head. She seeks the God who lifted her burdens and made her so glad. Even though her God is clothed in mystical garments and hides in the clouds, she insists, "I got something in me that speaks to God and hears from God."

God came, and comes, at his own time with invisible provisions. An angel told Hagar at the heat of her hurting: "God has heard your cry. Be not afraid. Take up the child and hold him up." When she turned with the boy in her arms God had placed a well of water for them to drink. The children of Hagar cry and are troubled along with their mother but God sees and hears and cares. He admonishes Hagar to hold up the child. Hagar's children are hurt, and conscious of the source of their hurt. Mothers, keep on praying and holding up our children! They may not seem like great potentials with miscegenation, miseducation, malnutrition of body and mind, but with God's help and your holding them up, they can make mountains of disadvantages into stepping stones to greatness. Never concede failure. It is so easy to fail in the struggle against great odds. However, it is a compliment to God's goodness and grace when we can wear the glorious crown of victory after conquering great odds. Keep holding up our children!

A great man, once speaking in a small town was forced to spend the night in a humble home where lived an uncouth boy and his mother. The boy did everything wrong and was an annoyance to this tremendous man. The next morning, with a sigh of relief, the man was on his way to more pleasant surroundings.

Many years passed and one evening this polite gentleman bought a box seat in a great auditorium to hear one of America's distinguished orators. He saw and heard this eminent young man speak with great eloquence, but there was a constant irritation in his mind—he kept thinking that he had met the speaker before. Upon greeting this young genius in the receiving line after the speech the gentleman asked if they had ever met. The young man said, "Yes, you were a guest in my home town many years ago when I was a small boy. You spent the night with my mother and me." The older man exclaimed: "You couldn't be the same boy! What happened?" The young man said in reply, "My mother loved me into what I am today." We must love our children and trust God for the results. Keep holding them up. Keep praying to God. Keep trusting God for his promises, keep believing that God will make a way. He will!

Greatness came to Ishmael as a leader and a man of great skills. We can easily point to the descendants of Hagar as great athletes. Ishmael introduces the use of the bow and arrow and becomes an expert archer. We do have the Goose Tatums and Julius Irvings (Dr. J.) of basketball and the Jim Browns and O. J. Simpsons of football. We do have the Joe Louises and Mohammed Alis of boxing. We are proud of the Jackie Robinsons and Hank Aarons of baseball. These are the gate openers for the all-time greats that go racing across the fields and floors of athletic competition today. But Aunt Hagar's children are not only in sports. They are presidents of colleges and universities with Booker T. Washington and Benjamin E. Mays. They are on the platforms with W.E.B. DuBois and Benjamin Hooks. They are in the pulpits with Gardner Taylor and J. H. Jackson. They are in the streets for freedom and justice for all men with Martin Luther King, Jr. and Jessie Jackson. They are singers with Marian Anderson and Mahalia Jackson, and poets with Paul Lawrence Dunbar and Langston Hughes. Aunt Hagar has children as mayors with Maynard Jackson, and congressmen with Walter Fauntroy, and ambassadors with Andrew Young. She has children everywhere and at all levels of society. Aunt Hagar's children have done well from basement parking-lot attendants to high-level executives. They found God in the deserts of their despair. And riding on the wings of Hagar's prayers they have soared to the loftiest peaks to live in the skies of success. All of Hagar's children are not there yet, but by God's grace we must keep pushing.

I am reminded of a story told by Dr. D. E. King of Monumental Baptist Church in Chicago, Illinois. He said that while attending the funeral of Dr. W. H. Jernigan at the Mount Carmel Baptist Church of Washington, D.C., he met a woman, a member of the entertainment committee, serving breakfast in the fellowship hall of the church. She was moaning to the music of her ancestors, somber but sweet sounds. It stirred the heart of Dr. King. He asked her, "Why are you singing like that?" She replied, "You wouldn't understand." Dr.

King said, "Tell me about it. You have filled me so until I don't feel I can eat my breakfast. Please tell me!"

Well, I had one son who promised to care for me all the days of my life. He gave me a place to stay with good furniture for my comfort. He gave me a clothing and food allowance. Everything went well until the first of this year when he was killed in an automobile accident. I went to God and told him that I wanted to die with my son. I asked God to let me bury my son and then to come for me that same night. Reverend, I lay on my bed knowing that God and I had made an agreement. Sleep came easy. Early the next morning I awakened, the room was the same, the chair, the window. Everything was the same. Strangely, though, I heard singing coming out of my pillow, on and under the bed:

> Be not dismayed whate'er betide,
> God will take care of you;
> Beneath His wings of love abide,
> God will take care of you!

I could not stay in bed, nor even in that room. I went to the bathroom and started to wash my dentures. As I turned on the water, the faucet said:

> Thro' days of toil when heart doth fail,
> God will take care of you;
> When dangers fierce your path assail
> God will take care of you.

I hurried out of the bathroom into the kitchen and began cooking breakfast. As soon as the pan got hot, instead of the bacon sizzling as usual, I heard from the pan:

> All you may need He will provide,
> God will take care of you;
> Nothing you ask will be denied,
> God will take care of you.

I turned away from the stove and sat in the living room. The walls seemed to sing the chorus of the song:

> God will take care of you,
> Thro' every day, O'er all the way;
> He will take care of you,
> God will take care of you.

While sitting there with tears in my eyes I faintly heard the doorbell ringing. Upon opening the door, I saw a young, well-dressed man standing on the porch. He said to me, "Your son worked for me and we became friends. I heard of his passing but I could not get here earlier, for my business carries me out of the country and around the world. However, your son told me that because of his working for me he was able to take care of you. He took out insurance on himself against this day. I have a check here for seven thousand dollars. I am leaving you my card with the check so you can reach me at any time. I am going to care for you as did your own son. Call whenever you need me." He turned and went down the steps to the street and got into a shining new automobile. As he turned the key and started the motor, I could hear the muffled roar of the automobile saying:

> No matter what will be the test,
> God will take care of you;
> Lean, weary one, upon His breast,
> God will take care of you.

Reverend, all night and all day angels keep watching over me.

Though misused and abused on this earth, we are assured that God will take care of us here and afterwhile. Every child of Hagar ought to trust God for the fruits of his promise.

THEY THAT WAIT FOR THE LORD

Assistant Professor of Theology
School of Religion
Howard University
Washington, D.C.

Thus saith the Lord God, . . . they shall not be ashamed that wait for me.

—Isaiah 49:22-23

During the Scripture reading, you might have felt disturbed by the prophet Isaiah's promise to those who wait for the Lord (Isa. 49:19-23). They shall not be ashamed, that is, defeated even when the jibes and the most withering rebuttal of their detractors and enemies have reduced them to laughingstocks. Does not our disturbance, actually our disquiet, hinge on more than a commitment to swift solutions to chronic personal and societal imbalances? What are we to make of the allegedly realistic view that the contradictions of life are irremediable? Father Henri Nouwen, the provocative Dutch Roman Catholic theologian on the faculty of the Yale Divinity School, has startlingly reminded us that our time is "a time in which it has become possible for man to destroy . . . not only man but also mankind, not only periods of existence but also history itself . . . the future has become an option."[1]

When one considers the enormous destructive potential of our creative powers, and glances sideways at the huge and ominous parentheses that this contradiction hurls around our fancied

[This sermon was preached in the Andrew Rankin Memorial Chapel of Howard University, Washington, D.C., on Sunday 26 September 1976. It is published here with minor editorial revisions.]

41

securities, the passage from Isaiah may sound like pious bogus. When one considers our perennial struggle to camouflage our naked frailties by impersonating God, so that even the best in us is constantly at the disposal of the demonic, it seems that Macbeth is right after all:

> Life's but a walking shadow, a poor player,
> That struts and frets his hour upon the stage,
> and then is heard no more; it is a tale
> Told by an idiot, full of sound and fury,
> Signifying nothing.

When one considers the long, unrequited travail of generations of the disinherited, now and again it seems that God is neither companion-in-misery nor enemy. Is the all-powerful and compassionate Ruler who occupies the throne of the universe an absentee? Who or what manages his estate—blind fate or the Devil? One thinks of Sterling A. Brown's poem, "Arkansas Chant":

> God may be the owner,
> But he's rich and forgetful,
> And far away.[2]

Such variations on a theme of trouble and disillusionment are not alien to the atmosphere of the Scriptures. Throughout the Book, the quest for God is depicted as a strange alternation of the sweetness of joy and the bitterness of an extraordinary sorrow.

You may recall John Donne's remarkable biblical insightfulness. Upon his return to London after a ruthless epidemic of the plague had befallen the city in 1625, he preached a most memorable sermon at Saint Paul's Cathedral, on 29 January 1926. Donne illustrated the tensions involved in waiting for the Lord as seen in their interplay in the terrible suffering of Job and Jesus.

Donne reminds us that as soon as we hear the Lord say he has found a blameless and upright man who fears God and opposes wrongdoing, we witness a commission to Satan to test the solidity of the man's faith. Lightning consumes Job's sheep and shepherds. Under Satan's blandishments roving bands of Sabeans despoil and plunder his oxen and asses and slay the herdsmen; Chaldeans raid his camels and waste the drivers. Fire and whirlwind crush his sons and daughters to death while they are feasting in the house of their eldest brother. Job is stricken with a loathsome disease. Just as Job's despair and fatigue are about to break his grip, he hasn't anyone to lean on for support.

Job—a man who had been eyes to the blind, feet to the lame, a father to the poor, a champion of the downtrodden—has become the laughingstock of cold, cruel, cynical young men who make him the butt of their songs. "Terrors are turned upon me," cries Job:

> . . . my honor is pursued as by the wind,
> and my prosperity has passed away like a cloud.

> . . . my soul is poured out within me;
> . . . .
> I cry to thee and thou dost not answer me;
> I stand, and thou dost not heed me.

Later we hear the confession of a sufferer for whom the dense darkness of trouble has become luminous:

> I know that thou canst do all things,
> and that no purpose of thine can be thwarted.
> . . . .
> I had heard of thee by the hearing of the ear,
> but now my eyes see thee;

As soon as we hear God say of the Master on the Mount of Transfiguration, "This is my beloved Son, with whom I am well pleased," our spirits are frozen, numbed, and eclipsed by a grim shadow of icy cynicism. We hear a tortured lament of abandonment at Calvary. The conspirators of darkness, the celebrants of the grotesque, have consolidated their rank in an effort to put Christ to an open shame. Look at them in their whirling, distempered madness. They are determined to push the strong Son of God into submission to their cause and to declare falsely the defeat of the cause for which he had come into the world. Is it any wonder that we hear the groans of a desperate soul, a cry erupting from the lonely depths of a love relationship of boundless trust and fidelity, "My God, my God, why hast thou forsaken me?" Is man the greatest weakness in this world? Is man's greatest fault being just and compassionate? Is man the most wretched of creatures? Is the righteous man the most miserable of men? And yet, somehow in the agony of his sorrow, in the aloneness of his heartbreak, his vision of God becomes most luminous. The Master cries, "Father, into thy hands I commend my spirit."

The waiting of which Isaiah speaks isn't a cowardly escape. Waiting is not wish-fulfillment, a denial of frustrated hope and labor, a flight of fancy from the boastful brutality of massive injustice. Waiting is not the naive expectation that power concedes without persistent demand. Ah, waiting *is* (to use William James's language) our confidence that "If this life be not a *real* fight, in which something is eternally gained for the universe by success, it is no better than a game of private theatricals from which one may withdraw at will. But it *feels* like a real fight. . . ."[3]

Nearly two weeks ago, Tuesday the fourteenth, funeral services were held in this sanctuary for our loved and lost Mordecai Wyatt Johnson.[4] The President drew heavily, and with touching eloquence, on one of Dr. Johnson's favorite Old Testament passages, the final verse of the fortieth chapter of the prophet Isaiah. President Cheek captured the quality of Dr. Johnson's faith in these words, "Looking back now upon the deeds he wrought, the works he brought forth, the lives he influenced, the legacies he left to all of us, we now know better than we knew before, that he waited upon the Lord and his strength was renewed, that he mounted up with wings as eagles, he ran and did not become weary, he walked and did not faint."[5]

At the conclusion of our ceremonies here, as with solemn pathos Dr. Johnson's bier was borne from this place, the University Choir sang as our recessional music the mighty "Hallelujah" chorus from Handel's *Messiah.* Later in the afternoon, as I sat reflecting on our act of thanksgiving, it occurred to me how immature and foolish and escapist and menacing our celebration of the Lord's faithfulness must have seemed to persons who insist that the meaning of life's offerings decays in the grave. Yet, even now, if I were to appeal to witnesses far and near, time would fail me to hear the testimonies of thousands upon thousands for whom our Lord is overcoming strength when life resembles a dark, chill, silent deadend street. And if life for you has grown "weary, stale, flat, and unprofitable," God will be your strength to see it through. I know it's a difficult saying, but something will be eternally gained.

We did not assemble in Rankin Chapel and in Cramton Auditorium merely to chronicle Dr. Johnson's remarkable achievements. What could have been more obscenely absurd than a pathetic recital (and nothing more!) of shining examples of the effectiveness Mordecai Johnson sustained even in spite of, and doubtless because of, the "doubting Thomases"? Dr. Benjamin Mays recalls in his autobiography, *Born to Rebel,* that the sceptics had wondered loud and long, Can a black man occupy successfully an office held formerly by white men? What were we doing here? Where life reaches out beyond the shallows, we were groping after an expression worthy of our heritage of faith, that all real living is waiting.

Waiting—not the resigned shudder of an oppressed creature. I speak of courageous defiance of the brazen conclusion that the dreams of the disinherited are forever against the drift of life. *Waiting*—not the solemn and consoling justification of the blood and tragedy of a heartless world. I speak of a radical reversal of an inner cynicism that dares starkly to assert that our struggle to *be* is a futile gesture in a universe without God. *Waiting*—the poised, robust confidence that something will be forever achieved for the universe not by our successes only, but by our faithfulness always, even if our noblest devotions have seemingly turned to dust. *Waiting*—another name for the quality of vision that comes of expectant involvement in the great issues of human destiny. For without a vision of liberated life, the soul of a man, of a woman, of a republic, of a university rots and pollutes the creative stream surrounding its gates.

I want you to listen again to the third stanza of our sermon hymn, George Matheson's "O Love That Wilt Not Let Me Go":

> O Joy that seekest me through pain,
> I cannot close my heart to thee;
> I trace the rainbow through the rain.
> And feel the promise is not vain
> That morn shall tearless be.

"Thus saith the Lord God, . . . they shall not be ashamed that wait for me." Are you able to testify to the Lord's faithfulness to his promise? I ask you again—are you? If you are, I urge you to renew your vow to the Lord, and live your life as the growing edge of his kingdom on earth, and never turn back. If you do not know whereof the prophet speaks, come and see, without delay, that all occasions invite God's mercies, that all times, the best of times and the worst of times, are his seasons.

NOTES

1. Henri J. M. Nouwen, *The Wounded Healer: Ministry in Contemporary Society* (New York: Doubleday & Co., 1972), p. 7.

2. Quoted in Jean Wagner, *Black Poets of the United States* (Urbana: University of Illinois Press, 1973), p. 692.

3. William James, "Is Life Worth Living?" *The Will to Believe* (New York: Dover Publications, 1956), p. 61.

4. The Reverend Dr. Mordecai W. Johnson (January 12, 1890—September 10, 1976), president emeritus of Howard University, Washington, D.C., was selected by the Board of Trustees on 30 June 1926 as the thirteenth president of the university. The first black scholar to assume the office of the Howard presidency since the founding of the university in 1867, Dr. Johnson's tenure lasted thirty-four years.

5. James E. Cheek, "A Tribute," in *New Directions: The Howard University* Magazine 4, no. 1 (January 1977): 13.

WHY DO THE RIGHTEOUS SUFFER?

CECIL WAYNE CONE

President of Edward Waters College
Jacksonville, Florida

> O Lord, how long shall I cry for help,
>   and thou wilt not hear?
> Or cry to thee "Violence!"
>   and thou wilt not save?
> Why dost thou make me see wrongs
>   and look upon trouble?
> Destruction and violence are before me;
>   strife and contention arise.
> So the law is slacked
>   and justice never goes forth.
> For the wicked surround the righteous,
>   so justice goes forth perverted.
>
>   —Habakkuk 1:2-4

One of the most perpetually perplexing mysteries of humankind is expressed in the question Why do the righteous suffer? This question is raised apart from the concern for the sufferings and misfortunes that exist in our world in general; for the pacifying answers of sin, wickedness, and natural disorders often find ready acceptance among humans in their eagerness to understand. But, for those who serve God, those who strive for the right, those who do others no harm, the Christians who suffer throughout history, the question is asked with increasing intensity "Why do the righteous suffer?"

This is a question that blacks, faced with the evils of slavery and oppression, have raised since first setting foot upon this foreign soil. This question is raised in light of the fact that God is worshipped within the black religious tradition as the Almighty Sovereign Creator and Sustainer of the world.

Viewing the sufferings of the past, the question is most pointedly phrased: "Why did God allow black people to suffer for 244 years in slavery and over another 100 years in racism and oppression?" The question was even raised during slavery itself. When black people found themselves in bondage, they delivered the total impact of their being against the stone wall of slavery. However, they soon discovered that they could not break that wall or even crack it. And yet, the slave could not resign himself to the condition of servitude. Thus, the slave found himself in a situation of extreme contradiction. The absurdity of this situation may be explained in this manner: On the one hand, the slave's understanding of himself as a human being would not allow him to become defined by the condition of slavery. But, on the other, he could not destroy slavery or escape from it. It was this contradiction that forced the black slave to recognize the finiteness of his own existence and being, thereby producing within the slave a sense of helplessness and despair.

This is graphically illustrated by the anguish expressed by Nathaniel Paul:

> Tell me, ye mighty waters, why did ye sustain the ponderous load of misery? Or speak, ye winds, and say why it was that ye executed your office to waft us onward to the still more dismal state; and, ye proud waves, why did you refuse to lend your aid and to have overwhelmed us with your billows? Then should we have slept sweetly in the bosom of the great deep and so have been hid from sorrow.[1]

Because the slave was not a determinist or fatalist, he had to address his complaint to God! If God and slavery are contradictions, as the slave felt in the essence of his being, why then are black people living in servitude? That is why Nathanial Paul wanted to know from God:

> And, oh thou immaculate God, be not angry with us, while we come into this thy sanctuary, and make the bold inquiry in this thy holy temple, why it was that thou didst look on with calm indifference of an unconcerned spectator when the holy law was violated, thy divine authority despised, and a portion of thine own creatures reduced to a state of mere vassalage and misery?[2]

Daniel Alexander Payne, a bishop in the African Methodist Episcopal Church, observing the sufferings of bondage and his own personal dilemma with respect to the absurdity of slavery raises the same concern by questioning the very existence of God:

> Sometimes it seemed as though some wild beast had plunged his fangs into my heart, and was squeezing out its lifeblood. Then I began questioning the existence of God, and saying: "If he does exist, is he just? If so, why does he suffer one race to oppress and enslave another, to rob them by unrighteous enactments of rights, which they hold most dear and sacred?"...Again, said I, "Is there no God"[3]

The question which is raised here by Bishop Payne is the theodicy question. The theodicy question addresses itself to reconciliation of God's omnipotence and intrinsic goodness in the midst of evil and suffering in the world. It asserts in answer to this theological dilemma, that either God is not all-powerful and thus unable to do anything about the evil in the world, or that he is not all just, and will not do anything about it. Addressing this dilemma, Bishop Payne is raising in essence the question "Why do the righteous suffer?"

As we approach this question, the first thing we should realize is that the Bible supports our right to raise this question. Job says in the midst of his agony, "Why are not times of judgment kept by the Almighty? And, why do those who know him never see his days?" Jeremiah asks, "Why, O God, does the righteous suffer?"

In the words of our text, Habakkuk raises the same question:

> O Lord, how long shall I cry for help,
>   and thou wilt not hear?
> Or cry to thee "Violence!"
>   and thou wilt not save?
> Why dost thou make me see wrongs
>   and look upon trouble?
> Destruction and violence are before me;
>   strife and contention arise.
> So the law is slacked
>   and justice never goes forth.
> For the wicked surround the righteous,
>   so justice goes forth perverted.
>
> (Hab. 1:2-4)

Habakkuk lived at a time when Judah was used as a shuttlecock by the great empires. First came the Assyrians, whose yoke of oppression was more than Judah could bear. Then came the Egyptians in 609 B.C. led by Necho, who not only invaded Judah but killed their young king, Josiah. Then, at the Battle of Carchemish in 605 B.C. Necho and his Egyptian army were defeated by Babylon led by Nebuchadrezzar II, who subsequently invaded Judah. Upon seeing all of these things, the young prophet Habbakuk raised the question, "Why dost thou [O God] look on faithless men, and art silent when the wicked swallows up the man more righteous than he?" (Hab. 1:13).

Habakkuk's complaint with God is not that Judah was so holy, but at least she was better than these nations that had invaded her land. This, of course, brings us to the point of the questions being raised within the black religious tradition concerning slavery and racism and oppression. It is not that black people are so holy and righteous as such, but as least they are better than the racist folk who have placed them under oppression.

There are various ways that people have attempted to solve the mystery of the sufferings of the righteous; but these answers inevitably fall into two categories: (1) God is limited. There is nothing he can do about the sufferings of his own. (2) God is not all-good. He just doesn't care.

Some philosophers like Edgar Sheffield Brightman and Peter Bertocci have introduced the idea of a defect in the being of God himself. That is to say, God is not all-powerful, but he is limited (though he is all-good), and evil exists in the world or the righteous suffer because God can do nothing about it. Still others have attempted to answer this question in terms that God is all-powerful, but he does not care. In the philosophical thinking of Newton and Boyle, the problem of evil is dismissed in the face of a more overall harmony in the world which outweights occasional disorders and anomalies. God is depicted as an intelligent Master Designer, a kind of Watchmaker who designs the world and winds it up like a clock and then sits back to watch. He only intervenes when and if something goes wrong, exercising his power in making adjustments as they occur in his created universe.

As with these philosophers, most of the historical answers to the problem of evil emphasize that either God is all-powerful and doesn't care, or he does care and is not all-powerful. This is what most human beings who are locked up in their own reasoning would say. Because human beings want to play God! They want to know! They want to have some rational answer. This is the same problem that Adam and Eve had—that's why they got thrown out of the garden. But, it's not just Adam and Eve's problem—it's not some problem back in history, it's our problem here and now. All of us want to play God! He has to fit within our little categories; and if he can't fit within our little categories, later for him! This is the most arrogant expression. We want proof of God's power, of his love, of his existence. When we find no such thing as proof, we are filled with despair.

What, then, is the Christian answer to this question, "Why do the righteous suffer?" The Christian answer is one which can only be found through an encounter with God. When Christians encounter God, they are totally overwhelmed by him. And being overwhelmed with this God, they deny themselves, take up their crosses, and follow him wherever he leads. The Christian answer is one which recognizes that there are some things that cannot be brought to a rational understanding because they transcend rationality. For, only "God knows the end from the beginning, and from ancient times things that are not yet done." The Christian answer is in harmony with the answer which Job received when he was complaining to God concerning the fact that God had set this world up wrong. God encounters Job in the midst of a whirlwind and raises some startling questions with him: "Where were you, Job, when I set the four corners of the universe? Where were you, when the morning stars sang together?" And, because of this encounter, Job recognizes his own finiteness, his own ignorance, his own limitations, his own nothingness in comparision with the Almighty Sovereign God. God alone has created this world and set it in order, and no little finite mind that is a speck on the cosmic wheel—Great God from Zion!—can dare comprehend what is going on in the cosmos rationally. And Job emerges from this experience crying, "I have heard of thee by the hearing of the ear (what other folks say about you), but now I see you face to face." And: "Though he slay me, yet will I trust him."

This is the answer with which Job comes out of his dilemma: "Though he slay me, yet will I trust him." It is because he had seen God face to face that he was able to come to this understanding.

The Christian answer, too, is one that is in harmony with the answer Habakkuk received: "The just shall live by faith." Not by sight—not by rationality. Habakkuk's encounter with God leads him to conclude:

> Though the fig tree do not blossom,
>> nor fruit be on the vines,
> the produce of the olive fail
>> and the fields yield no food,
> the flock be cut off from the fold
>> and there be no herd in the stalls,
> yet I will rejoice in the Lord,
>> I will joy in the God of my salvation.
> God, the Lord, is my strength;
>> he makes my feet like hinds' feet,
>> he makes me tread upon my high places.
>
> (Hab. 3:17-19)

The Christian answer is consistent with the answer in the black tradition. The black tradition is not rational, but based upon an experience of divine encounter with the Almighty Sovereign God. Now, when the black slave found himself in the awful condition of slavery where resistance was only an option at a minimal level, and in a situation where he refused to resign himself to the condition of servitude, this contradiction drove the slave to the very edge of despair, or as one writer put it: "Down where prayer is hardly more than a moan, down there close where life and death seem almost equatable." But in this absurd situation, the slave encountered the Almighty Sovereign God. The God the slave encountered was not the God of white missionaries, but the God of his lost African heritage, and of his own experience, who was more powerful than the slave traders and overseers. This experience of the divine and the recognition that God was greater and more powerful than the laws of slavery created excitement and joy in the very being of the slave. That is why he sang:

> He's so high you can't go over him,
> He's so low you can't go under him,
> He's so wide you can't go around him,
> You've got to go right through the door.

This experience of God in the midst of slavery did not blind the slave to his condition of slavery even though he recognized that God was more powerful than slavery itself. But it gave him the strength and ability to rise above the contradictions of his existence. It gave him the kind of faith and understanding of God that Job had, when he cried, "Though he slay me, yet will I trust him," and that Habakkuk had when he concluded:

> Though the fig tree do not blossom,
>   nor fruit be on the vines,
> the produce of the olive fail
>   and the fields yield no food,
> the flock be cut off from the fold
>   and there be no herd in the stalls,
> yet I will rejoice in the Lord,
>   I will joy in the God of my salvation.
>
> (Hab. 3:17-18)

That is why the slave in the midst of his sorrow, in the absurdity of slavery was able to sing praises to God through the spirituals. This encounter with the Almighty Sovereign God, although it did not immediately end the slave's external condition of suffering, enabled him to maintain a sense of well-being in the daily misery of his existence. With the kind of faith that contradicts rationality that we have observed in the expressions of Job and Habakkuk, the encounter with God enabled the slave to sing:

> Nobody knows the troubles I see,
> Nobody knows but Jesus.
> Nobody knows the troubles I see,
> Glory, Hallelujah!

NOTES

1. Carter G. Woodson, *Negro Orators and Their Orations* (Washington: Associated Publishers, 1925), p. 69.
2. Ibid.
3. "Document: Bishop Daniel Alexander Payne's Protestation of American Slavery," - *Journal of Negro History* 52, no. 63 (1967): 27.

PART TWO

NEW TESTAMENT THEMES

THE SUFFERING GOD

EDWARD P. WIMBERLY

Assistant Professor of Pastoral Care
Interdenominational Theological Center
Atlanta, Georgia

> At three o'clock Jesus cried out with a loud shout, "Eloi, Eloi, lema sabachthani?" which means, "My God, my God, why did you abandon me?
>
> —Mark 15:34(TEV)

Good Friday brings the question of evil and suffering into sharp focus for us. The problem of the why of suffering has challenged humankind since the beginning of our existence here on earth. But Good Friday seems to raise the question poignantly in human history once again. Jesus, the carpenter's son—a healer of sickness, an expeller of evil spirits, and a bearer of good news—was killed in order to let a known criminal go free. My mind cannot imagine what could have been in the mind of the crowd that day when they deliberately chose injustice over justice, evil over good, and suffering over against healing. Yes, Jesus was like a lamb led to slaughter and like a sheep who made no noise before his shearers. Why is suffering allowed to happen like this? We examine this question in our hearts every day.

Suffering takes many forms in our lives. I think of the great earthquakes that have killed thousands of persons, crushing them under thousands of pounds of earth. I think of the monstrous injustices suffered by innocent victims during slavery and during Hitler's reign on this earth. I think of the many deaths suffered every day because of the incompleteness of medical knowledge. We as Christians are in great error when we falsely conclude that all the suffering in the world is due to sin and humanity's feeble choices. Yes, injustice is a result of sin, but Paul talks not only of sin; he talks of evil being death, principalities, and powers (Rom. 8:38). For Paul there were destructive forces in the world running independent of sin, and these forces caused just as much misery to the lives of persons as sin. Even death was an evil for Paul. There was nothing good about the fact that man must die. He saw the whole of God's creation in need of salvation. The whole world was groaning for salvation and liberation according to Paul (Rom. 8:19-23).

If, indeed, the world was in need of salvation, did not God create the world? Doesn't this mean that God can't be all-powerful? You may also ask another question: If God is all-loving, how can we reconcile this with the suffering and evil in the world? Surely, God is responsible in some way.

I don't propose to examine all the theories of why God permits suffering in the world. As the writer of the Book of Job points out, God's ways cannot be fully grasped through reason. In order to fully grasp the problem of evil and human suffering in the world, one needs to employ both faith and reason.

What does faith tell us about suffering? Faith, as a response to what God has done for us in our struggle with suffering, is a belief that God is at work in our lives helping us struggle with the consequences of suffering. Faith is believing that God has not left us alone to struggle with the devastation of suffering. Whether suffering is the result of natural disaster, sin, oppression, or death, God is working in our lives trying to help us overcome, overthrow, and live in spite of it. Our faith tells us that God does not like suffering, and he is doing all he can to help us. Moreover, God is at work trying to eliminate suffering from this world.

Faith tells us that God is a suffering God. I would like to examine this faith statement by using an example from pastoral experience. There was a young woman lying in her hospital bed grief-stricken because she was not able to produce life in this world. She was suffering the despair of losing a child through miscarriage that she had nurtured in her womb for six months. Her pain was deep, and it could not be swept away by shallow words of condolence.

Her pain was anchored deep in her soul. Not long after she and her husband had rejoiced over the news that she was pregnant she lost her husband in a tragic car accident. She almost lost the baby in her agony, but she was able to hold on for five months. However, just when she was recovering from the loss of her husband another loss was inflicted upon her.

Sometimes, as we all know, tragedy comes in threes. You say nothing more could happen to her. Oh I wish that were so, but life had one more monstrous episode for her to face. While in the hospital for the miscarriage the doctors discovered she had a malignant tumor in her breast, and they had to do radical surgery in order to remove the cancer. What a cruel trick life was playing on her. I don't blame you if you find this series of unfortunate events unbelievable. It is incredible to sustain such losses in such a short period of time.

During this woman's stay in the hospital, she was visited by the hospital chaplain. As she slowly recounted her sad story to the chaplain tears came streaming down her cheeks forming a small puddle of water in her lap. Her voice was very low, and it cracked periodically because she was so weak; she could hardly form words with her lips, indicating her remorse was emerging deep from within.

The chaplain found himself caught in the gloomy depression of the woman. He could feel her great sadness within his own heart. He suddenly found himself fighting back his tears as if he himself had sustained a terrible loss. He was vicariously experiencing what she was feeling. The chaplain, as a result, felt the need to say a word of condolence and chose a very unfortunate phrase. He said, "I understand how you feel." Of course he was feeling what the woman was feeling through contagion, but it was not quite the same thing. At the moment he uttered these words the woman cried out with a loud voice and with an angry look on her face, "What do you mean you understand? Have you ever lost a wife? Have you ever lost a child? Have you ever been told you were going to lose your manhood? No one understands me." Realizing his tactical mistake the chaplain responded: "You have a right to be angry with me. You have a right to be angry at the world."

This chaplain's last response to the grief-stricken woman is very instructive for our understanding of the meaning of the phrase "the suffering God." Rather than withdrawing from the woman in fear of her anger, the chaplain sought to identify and enter the anger of the woman. His response, "you have a right to be angry at me," was an invitation by the chaplain for the grieving woman to project her hostility onto him. In this way he hoped to help her not keep inside her the negative, bitter feelings associated with being abandoned. This would help her do her grieving so she could get over this period of mourning and return to an active life again. This willingness to enter the woman's pain in order to help her with it forms a good analogy of how God becomes a suffering God to help us with our suffering. In fact, I can say, God was actually working in the chaplain to help this woman to live in spite of and to overcome her pain. It was not the chaplain who said, "It is all right to be angry." But, working through the chaplain, it was God himself who uttered the words. God became a suffering God by entering the woman's pain.

Indeed, God is a suffering God. This was made clear on Good Friday when Jesus cried out in great agony, "My God, My God, why hast thou forsaken me?" In this cry of abandonment, in this passionate plea Jesus was expressing his oneness with humanity. It was at this moment that God was in Christ suffering in order to point the way for us in our suffering. It was God's way of saying, "I have been there too; please allow me to show you the way out of your suffering." It was God's way of saying, "Let me help you carry your burdens just a little while." Yes, God is a suffering God. He has not left us alone. He has shown us he cares what happens to us.

Some of you may be asking, "Why is the concept of a suffering God so important?" A student asked me this question one day in class as I was struggling to explain what I meant by the concept. The student was very direct and forceful. He said, "This concept of the suffering God was not adequate for me. I just cannot quite understand a concept which allows my God to be weak and suffering. My God must not be weak, he must be strong."

At the time I felt that this student was not asking an academic question, but was searching very hard to understand my faith statement. So I asked him to look at the biblical record and read the accounts of the incarnation, the passion, and the death of Jesus. I was hoping that this student would discover that it was not just *my* concept of the suffering God but that God himself chose suffering as his way of reconciling the world to himself.

When God chose to be a suffering God, I can imagine that he had a long dialogue with himself. I can picture in my mind that God was saying, "What would be the best way to once and for all communicate my love and concern to my beloved children?" I can visualize God weighing in his mind whether or not he would remain remote and distant from the involvement of humankind against the forces of evil. But, I thank God the result of his self-dialogue was that he chose to divest himself of his divine power temporarily so that he could empathetically enter into our suffering and pain.

I am sure God's dialogue with himself included some understanding of human nature. Perhaps, if I can be so bold to suggest it: human beings would not trust a God who would not involve himself with suffering and pain. Somehow I feel God knew we would not believe in his goodness if he did not engage himself personally with evil.

Let me illustrate what I am talking about: There was an elderly woman who was completely dissatisfied with my being appointed to the church by the bishop. I was a young, twenty-five-year-old just out of seminary. She protested to the district superintendent that I was too young, and had no experience. She felt that her pastor needed to have experienced life and struggled triumphantly over some of his personal problems in order to be her pastor. She wanted someone who had tasted the bittersweetness of life and who could transalte this bittersweetness into joy and hope. Clearly, age and experience alone could provide such an education.

God knew we all were like this woman. He knew that as long as he remained remote and distant from the problems we faced, we would find all kinds of excuses to ignore his goodness. It is very true that we must know personally that someone is able to understand our suffering and pain before we allow him or her a place in our lives. Henri Nouwen graphically points out in *The Wounded Healer* that we are indeed a people who would not see God as authentic unless his caring came from a "heart wounded by suffering." Nouwen goes on to say, "No God can save us except a suffering God" (p. 72). He continues: "Who can save a child from a burning house without taking the risk of being hurt by the flames? Who can listen to a story of loneliness and despair without the risk of experiencing similar pains in his heart. In short; who can take away suffering without entering it?" (pp. 72-73).

The concept of a suffering God is important because we would not feel that God really cared for us unless he was willing to enter our pain. In the incarnation God declared his willingness to enter and suffer the same consequences of evil that we face every day. In becoming human he was saying, "You are valuable to me, and I will be willing to risk my own life for you." He was saying, "I want to show you I really understand what you are facing in life."

Because God entered life most of us take him very seriously. Moreover, because God has entered life we find ourselves profoundly understood at the depth of our being. This was the testimony of the woman at the well who cried out after encountering Jesus, "Come see a man who told me everything I ever did." Another way of saying this would be, "Come see a man who understands me in a way no one else understands me." Yes, God chose to be a suffering God so that he might communicate to us his love and concern. Only a suffering God can understand what we have to put up with here on earth.

God has suffered what you and I have suffered. He has been rejected in his own home. He has been ridiculed in public. He has been knocked down and walked on as a doormat. He was betrayed by loved ones. He was oppressed by the power structure. He was put to death by enemies. All this for us.

And not only is God a suffering God; he is an able God. God suffers but he is not weak. Our God has experienced the agony of pain, but he has not been reduced to inactive helplessness. Our God has exerienced the sinking despair that evil produces in life, but he has not been drowned or overcome by it. God is able.

God is able to enter into our pain and suffering caused by the devastating powers of evil. But God can do more than this. He can help us find resources to help us live meaningful and triumphant lives in spite of the threatening hand of suffering. God's shoulders are broad enough to carry our burdens until our strength is sufficient to shoulder them ourselves. When suffering shuts doors of opportunity in our face and oppression keeps the doors to fulfillment shut, God is able to find the key to help us unlock the closed doors. When the storms of life are raging and our lives are being dashed upon the sharp, jagged rocks, God is able to command the winds and the waves to be silent and still. Our God may suffer, but like all suffering it is only temporary. God is able.

We as black people have often wondered why we have had to suffer the injustices of racism here in America. I can say at this time that I don't believe God intends for anyone to suffer. But sin, man's separation from God, can cause man to enslave his fellowman and cause grave consequences to the image of God in all humans. I know that evil, suffering, and oppression exist, and God never promised us that we would not have to face the problems of evil. We face them with faith and with hope because he entered into this world, because he suffers with us in our suffering, and because he is able.

THE BOLD ONES

MANCE C. JACKSON

Director of Continuing Education for Black Clergy
Interdenominational Theological Center
Atlanta, Georgia

Now when they saw the boldness of Peter and John, and perceived that they were uneducated, common men, they wondered.

—Acts 4:13

Evil and suffering are among the many "givens" experienced in life. All persons reflect evil of scme kind in their lives during their lifetime and all persons are victims of evil more than any of us can accurately assess. Whether intentionally or unintentionally, each of us is directly responsible for a great deal of suffering experienced by those who live close to us. And the suffering caused by those who are powerful among us leaps over mountains and oceans to people in distant lands. By the same token, each of us experiences the excruciating pain of suffering. Many of us live it in our bodies as a constant companion. Some of us know it as a nagging heartache, born out of grief over the loss of a loved one, or out of the terrible loneliness which dogs our heels wherever we turn. To mention these forms of evil and suffering is to acknowledge that there is a host of channels through which evil and suffering flow.

In this message, I want to focus on a dimension of evil and suffering, which like violent conflict, has plagued the human family since the beginning of time. In their narrowness and selfishness people have built barriers around themselves in an attempt to separate themselves from their neighbors who may be different in some way. Racial hatred, racial prejudice and racial oppression are vicious forms of evil, and the suffering which they impose on others is unhuman to say the least.

Black people in America have suffered and will suffer for years to come the effects of this historical human tragedy. As we reflect on the evil and suffering which we have experienced in the past, and as we face an uncertain future in a shrinking, racist, highly nationalistic, technologically advancing, resource-depleting world, we must take some steps as a people which will help us face the evil and suffering ahead of us.

Numerous suggestions come to us in this regard from the biblical stories. In this message I will share three of those suggestions with you:

1. An oppressed people must boldly worship their liberating God.

The story in our text describes what happens to people who have experienced the liberating power of God. Peter and John and all of the believers in Christ in Jerusalem had great personal and spiritual power because they glorified God's presence in their midst.

Historically, black people in America have acknowledged that our deliverance from bondage was the work of the Lord. Like all people, our foreparents in slavery had deep longings and passionate desires to stand as equals alongside of their neighbors. But they had no arms, no materials, no economy and no political means for enabling their own emancipation. The only things they had were their halting, feeble prayers and their belief in a just and righteous God. They knew that their heavenly Father saw the evil being perpetrated against them, and they knew that he shared their suffering with them even as he had shared it with his Son Jesus when he prayed in the garden of Gethsemane. They also knew that their only hope for freedom rested in his divine intervention. Historians who write that the Civil War was fought primarily to preserve the Union have no understanding of how God works to effect justice among men. God acted in the person of Abraham Lincoln and ended an era of evil that gripped this land. What learned historians fail to understand, ignorant ex-slaves understood with the keenest of insight. The result was that they boldly and faithfully worshipped the God who acted on their behalf.

The memory of God's intervention on our behalf has grown faint.

For many of our people, the story has lost its relevance. They have forgotten the God who liberated us from the evil of slavery and gave us the opportunity to serve him in freedom. Experiencing the drama of his power in the act of their emancipation, our foreparents knew God as a great God, a victorious God, a merciful, saving God. He was real to them because they had witnessed his triumphant defeat of the evil of slavery and they adored and worshipped him.

Our God has brought us a long way since that time. Indeed, he has brought us in spite of ourselves. Our memories are not long. We soon forget how we got where we are. And we lose access to the power which sustained former generations of our people. Like Peter and John and those in the early church, our foreparents knew the source of the power we need. They stayed close to the source and had remarkable achievements as a result. If we are to have the power we need to achieve the goals challenging our generation, we must boldly worship him who liberated us then and who sustains us now.

2. An oppressed people must be bold to claim their liberation.

In the dialogue that went on between Peter and John and the established leaders, Peter and John had to boldly claim their right to obey God rather than men. Just a few days before, the same group of men had condemned Jesus to death. His followers could have been greatly intimidated, even immobilized by such power. Something happened to them on the day of Pentecost however. God came to them in the fullness of his power. He took away their fears and empowered them to boldly claim their liberation from those who would restrain and oppress them.

Physical emancipation is a fact for Afro-Americans. The shackles have been removed from our legs and slave-catchers no longer ride to contain us on given plantations. But after more than one hundred years of physical freedom, the evil of slavery is still with many of us. The shackles are on our minds. Our emancipation is not yet consummated.

The condition of our continuing enslavement expresses itself in many ways. One way is in the limited responsibility which we assume for the communities in which we live. In many of the towns, cities and counties across this country, black people are the racial majority in the population. Yet they do not vote in sufficient numbers to elect leadership which will represent their interests.

A second and related way in which our continuing enslavement manifests itself is in the attitudes of so many of our people toward black leadership. Many of us have been taught and therefore continue to think that anything black is inferior, including community leadership. It naturally follows then that the masses of our people in some communities think that political offices are places for "white only." In one central Georgia county where blacks make up nearly eight percent of the population, there is no black elected official at the county level. In discussing the matter with local black residents, they stated that black people are not yet ready for such positions. In the decade of Maynard Jackson, Tom Bradley, Shirley Chisholm, Andrew Young, Barbara Jordan, Coleman Young and others too numerous to name, our slave mentality tells some of us that black people are not yet capable of assuming responsibility for public office!

A third way through which our enslavement expresses itself is in our apathy toward the physical conditions in which we live. Granted, we inherit residential communities which whites have abandoned, many of which are already deteriorating. And granted, our economic resources are not adequate to keep old dwellings in good repair. But we can put our cans, bottles and paper in trash cans instead of discarding them wherever we happen to be. We can mow lawns regularly and pull the weeds around our homes. We can have abandoned cars removed from our neighborhoods and trash removed from the blocks where we live. We can organize ourselves into neighborhood improvement groups and block clubs for the purpose of making our environment a more wholesome place for living.

We must affirm our liberation. We are a free people. We are free in Christ Jesus our Lord. And when one is free in Christ, one is free indeed. Let us boldly wrest the shackles from our minds. Let us put off the old man and put on the new man—the bold, free man.

3. An oppressed people must boldly strive to change systems which perpetuate their oppression.

According to the way the record reads in our text, Peter and John were arrested for preaching the doctrine of the resurrection in

Jesus Christ. Since the doctrine of the resurrection was held by the Pharisees, some of whom were numbered among the established leadership, the doctrine was not the issue in the arrest. The promotion of Jesus and his teachings was the issue, along with the favorable response being given by the people. The authorities evidently felt that their base of support would be threatened in some way by a grassroots movement towards the teachings of Jesus. Their way of dealing with the perceived threat was by harassing the followers of Jesus with undue arrests and mock trials such as Jesus had been given.

Such tactics seem to follow the oppressed down through the ages. If it appears that their eyes may be opened to ways of relieving some of their suffering, the evil in their oppressors comes forth with all its vicious cruelty. Every bitter option they can think of is surfaced for consideration in order to keep the oppressed "in their place," in their condition. Harassing their leaders with false arrests, unfair legal judgments and prolonged jail and prison sentences are some of the first steps.

Among the many systems which black people in America must boldly act to change is "the criminal justice system." It is the conclusion of many social analysts that in this society the police and sheriff departments, the jails, the prisons, the attorneys, the judges, and the courts they administer are designed to protect the interest of the wealthy and to contain the oppressed so that they do not make waves for their oppressors.

Changing the criminal justice system must be a priority concern for oppressed people because of what it does to them mentally, psychologically, physically, socially, economically, and spiritually. Large numbers of our young men have arrest records and are serving in prisons for ordinary adolescent behavior. They have committed no crimes worth noting. But they are black, and more often than not they are poor. In the jails and prisons they grow angry, cold and bitter over unjust treatment and they return to their communities determined to get even with society for the mistreatment received. Unfortunately their loved ones become the objects of their hostilities. They disrespect the intimate relationships which they establish with young women. They desert their families and the responsibilities related to family living. In their self-pity they seek escape from their suffering through the use of drugs, alcohol, illicit and deviant sexual activity. For minor legal infractions many black men are driven to despair, their families are shattered and their futures destroyed simply because they were born with a skin color different from that of their neighbors. We must be bold to change a system which is so criminal in its effects on people.

Many of the judicial seats are elective offices. The others are filled by political appointment. One way that we can change the criminal justice system is by voting and electing to office persons who think and feel as we do about the system. Mayors, governors, and presidents elected to office with strong black support must be made sensitive to black concerns in the making of appointments to offices such as those of police chief and judge. Another way that we can change the system is by making those in positions of authority accountable to the community they serve. We must be bold and strive to change the criminal justice system and all other systems which tend to perpetuate our oppression.

Peter and John were uneducated, common men, but they acted boldly. From their story we take heart to worship and witness with courage. Where evil, suffering, and oppression are concerned, boldness is clearly in order.

OUR FATHER, THE KING

JOHN R. BRYANT

Minister of Bethel African Methodist Episcopal Church
Baltimore, Maryland

The Spirit itself beareth witness with our spirit, that we are the children of God: And if children, then heirs; heirs of God, and joint-heirs with Christ; if so be that we suffer with him, that we may be also glorified together. For I reckon that the sufferings of this present time are not worthy to be compared with the glory which shall be revealed in us.

—Romans 8:16-18

Our God is a mystery! He is everywhere at the same time. He's a mystery. One writer has said God is so high above us we cannot reach him. He is so deep within us we cannot escape from him. Our God is a mystery. He testified of himself: "My thoughts are not your thoughts, . . . For as the heavens are highter than the earth, so are my ways highter than your ways and my thoughts than your thoughts." Our God is a mystery. The hymnist pondered him and penned:

> God moves in a mysterious way
> His wonders to perform;
> He plants his footsteps in the sea,
> And rides upon the storm.

The mystery of God's nature is heightened the more when we consider how he treats his children. Society's description of a good parent is one that protects, inspires, disciplines (not harshly), provides material needs and wants, and cushions from the rough places in life. If a child is fortunate enough to have parents that are wealthy, that child goes without want. To be the child of a president or king is to experience a life of comfort and ease. Our Father is king, but remember he is also a mystery: Our God has a strange notion about how his children ought to live. Some of the experiences God allows us to have are to help make us a special people. Our Father wants us to love when hated, to stand when knocked down, and to serve—not to be served.

In order to prepare his children to live life properly, the Father will sometimes lead his children into danger. Sometimes he'll walk them through the very "valley of the shadow of death," in order to teach them to "fear no evil," for he is with them. He wants them to learn that he brings some through the water, some through the flood, some through the fire, but *all* through the blood. God leads his dear children along.

The best contemporary example of how God deals with his children is found in the saga of the black man's sojourn in North America. The story of the black man's life in America ought to be read and pondered by blacks and whites alike. This story has been told by great minds like Frederick Douglass, Henry McNeal Turner, Richard Allen, Benjamin Quarles, Marcus Garvey, Carter G. Woodson, W. E. B. DuBois, A. J. Rogers, Alex Haley, and the list continues. Many have been exposed to this story and concluded that black Americans are poor orphans. How wrong they are: we are "children of the King." Yes, black folk have "known rivers" and, yes, life for them has not been a crystal star, but still they are able to affirm: "We are children of the King." It's hard for folk to believe this when they hear the black story. It's a bittersweet story. The story is full of suffering, pain, sacrifice, and oppression. It's the story of a proud people stolen from the shores of Africa. The story tells of them being whipped, chained, humiliated, lynched, hated, tarred and feathered.

Through all the torture and pain, on every page of each chapter, the same name has always been found on their lips. The name of the word has been a constant in the community of these children in Africa. On chain gangs they chanted *Lord;* from cotton patches they wailed for *God*; in secret churches in the woods they shouted *Jesus*; in welfare and unemployment lines they moan *Father*. Many have seen our loyalty to God in the very face of suffering and concluded that our God was deaf or dead, or did not care. Folk have thought that way, and continue to think that way simply because they don't understand our Father, the King.

In order to understand our story you have to understand something about the nature of God. One must know that God very often works through his children in making the world a better place. God's use of his children often requires that they suffer in the process. The suffering is redemptive, for it is in keeping with the will of God. Abraham had to go through the trauma of almost sacrificing his own son so the world might know that God must come first. Job had to suffer physical affliction so that the world might know, "He may not come when you want him, but he's always on time." The Hebrews had to struggle for forty years in the wilderness so we might learn that only the faithful are delivered. Martin Luther King, Jr. had to experience an early death so men everywhere might know that evil men may destroy the dreamer, but they cannot destroy the dream.

When the Father decides to use his children, he equips them for survival. When God works with man he prepares man. God prepares man through the process of a second birth. Man's first birth is a birth in the flesh. Man in the flesh suffers—he is oppressed, enslaved, abused, and even murdered. So that the suffering the children of God experience may not be ultimate, there is a second birth. Yes, the first birth is of the flesh, and the second birth is of the spirit. The second birth gives the children of God power over the flesh. As a result of the two births you may enslave one's flesh, but his spirit sets him free! You may tell me in the flesh, because I'm black, I'm nobody—but my spirit tells me, "I'm a child of the King!"

Paul tried to tell the church at Rome that they were heirs of God. Paul wanted them to know that though they would be persecuted, they must always remember they were heirs of God. He wanted them to know that though they may be thrown in the lions' den, or even imprisoned, they were heirs of God. Paul's message is for us today: Never mind your circumstance or your day-to-day suffering, you are heirs of God. You may be unemployed; maybe your health is poor; maybe you are a victim of discrimination—always remember you are a child of God.

There are those who will want to know how much will they have to suffer. Do you want to know how much God's children have to bear? For the answer we only have to look at the life of our elder brother: "For God so loved the world, that he gave his only begotten Son, that whosoever believeth in him should not perish, but have everlasting life." Jesus was sent by the Father to suffer, bleed, and die for the sins of the world. Being in the same family, Paul declares in the eighth chapter of Romans that we are joint heirs with Christ. We are partners in the suffering of life crucifixions, but praise be to God—we are also joint heirs with him in the Father's resurrection.

Though we suffer in this life, we must remember that the glory is better than the suffering. When the weight of my suffering begins to overpower, it gives me strength to remember the reckoning of Paul, that "the sufferings of this present time are not worthy to be compared with the glory which shall be revealed in us." (Rom. 8:18). In other words, "Weeping may endure for a night, but joy cometh in the morning." So, "Walk together, children, don't you get weary, . . ."

WHAT CAN CHRISTIANITY DO FOR ME?

THOMAS HOYT, JR.

Assistant Professor of New Testament
Interdenominational Theological Center
Atlanta, Georgia

For ye suffer fools gladly, seeing ye yourselves are wise. . . . And he said unto me, My grace is sufficient for thee: for my strength is made perfect in weakness. Most gladly therefore will I rather glory in my infirmities, that the power of Christ may rest upon me.

—2 Corinthians 11:19; 12:9

"Religion can make you healthy, wealthy, and wise" is a slogan heard constantly these days. One can hardly turn on the radio, view the television, or attend one's church without hearing that reverberating slogan. For many, religion has become what Karl Marx called "an opiate for the masses." This is not to say that Christianity does not offer its followers something. That's the devilish thing about those charlatans today who are offering God to persons on the basis that such takers will increase their personal health, comfort, and security.

The devilish thing about this promise is that Christianity may well offer these things and more. It is when the promise is made the purpose of belief in God that our religion become blasphemous. There are a lot of people today getting interested in Jesus Christ and the "born again" movement simply because of what it can do for them. All half-truths are devilish. We need to place in proper perspective this modern tendency to extol Christianity on the basis of what it offers for our use as opposed to what God wishes to do through his use of us.

The Apostle Paul had to recount some factors in his life that are helpful in setting the record straight for Christian discipleship. He gives us a bit of autobiographical data in relationship to a dispute in the Corinthian church.

There was a controversy in the church at Corinth where some had questioned Paul's authority. Others had claimed that their right to lead the church was more legitimate than his. "All right, then," says, Paul in effect. "Look here, you force me to act like a fool; so, let me tell you what Christianity has done for me. Others are boasting; let me have 'my little boast,' also." And so, Paul wrote a severe letter to these friends. We believe a part of that letter is found in 2 Corinthians 10-13.

In the first place, it is crystal clear that Christianity, rather than keeping Paul out of trouble, got him into a whole bundle of it. There is not need to list every single item in the long series of trials and tribulations. Just look at Paul's experiences should cause reassessment for those who bemoan how harshly life has treated them.

Following Jesus cost him hard work, of course. But beyond that there were floggings, a half dozen of them. He was stoned, thrown into jail and shipwrecked; he suffered from cold and exposure and flirted constantly with death. All this and more happened not by chance or accident, we are led to presume, but directly as a result of his religious commitment to his Lord and Master.

Even beyond the physical sufferings went a suffering of mind and spirit too. Paul did not get out of Christianity peace of mind and soul in any shallow sense. He had sleepless nights. There came an added sensitivity to the plight of others: "Who is weak and I am not weak? Who is offended and I burn not?" There came additional burdens from the churches in his care. Instead of Christianity getting him out from under difficulties, it really pushed him under far more problems than he had ever had before. As if his own troubles were not enough, he found himself loaded down with the problems of others.

Our look at Paul, thus far, suggests that Christianity gave him a singularly rough time of it: headaches, heartaches and physical abuses. It suggests rather strongly that you and I may well expect our being "born again" to get us *into* trouble rather than *out* of it.

We don't have to go out to glorify suffering. We don't have to go out and make martyrs of ourselves. We don't have to search, as some did during the early centuries of the Christian movement, for crowns of thorns so as to prove to ourselves and the world that we are faithful followers of Christ. It is true that there are Christians who, like Paul, have been in prisons and in peril of death simply because they were faithful in their Christian convictions. You and I may not be called on for a similar witness; circumstances will determine that. At the very least, however, we may expect religion to get us into trouble.

My former homiletics professor made some comments on the slogan that the Christian religion is a "storm in a golden frame." He thinks the image needs to be reversed. The storm is not the center. The storm develops around the edges where God and his will come into contact with human life.

If one listens attentively to the weather reports, one knows that when clear, cold, refreshing air comes down from Canada and hits a mass of hot, humid, stagnant air, storms develop along the edges of the cold front, often with lightning, thunder, and torrential rains. God's invasion in our world brings storms into the human scene. True, God offers us rest and peace but he often has to make us restless before he can give us rest. If we are to be ambassadors or agents of God in the world, we can expect some sufferings. If not actual physical sufferings like those of Jesus, Paul, and Martin Luther King, Jr., we can expect at least a conscience sensitized to the injustices of others. A Christian cannot ever merely watch in the stands the sufferings and torture of others without empathizing and seeking to alleviate those sufferings in the arenas of life.

Being born again certainly did not cut down on Paul's physical sufferings inflicted on him by others. Neither were his spiritual sufferings which developed out of his concern for the church any the less as a result of his new birth. We are thereby warned against expecting life to be easy as a result of being a Christian. But that's not all.

Christianity offers the presence of God. In the midst of the sufferings Paul speaks of visions and revelations of the Lord. Rather than Christianity being a storm in a golden frame, Paul would place God at the center of the frame and the storms on the fringes. This attitude is in tune with the old Negro gospel hymn "When the Storms of Life Are Raging, Stand by Me." It is in rhythm with the promise of Jesus in John 14:27 "Peace I leave with you; my peace I give to you; not as the world gives do I give to you." The kind of peace Jesus offers is not that found in the absence of war but the calm in the midst of turmoil. It is the kind of peace that compelled Martin Luther King, Jr. to sacrifice his life for the rights of the oppressed and to say:

> . . . I don't know what will happen now. We have got difficult days ahead. But it doesn't matter with me because I've been to the mountaintop. Like anyone else, I would like to live a long life. But I'm not concerned with that. I just want to do God's will and he has allowed me to go up the mountain. I've seen the promised land. I may not get there with you, but I want you to know tonight that we as a people will get to the promised land. I am happy tonight that I am not worried about anything. I'm not fearing any man. "Mine eyes have seen the glory of the coming of the Lord."

Christianity does not offer a painkiller; it offers victory. In talking of his visions and great experiences with God, Paul's head could have gotten swelled, but it didn't. You understand why it did not? There was this thorn in the flesh. We never have known what the thorn was. There have been many ideas and opinions about it. Some people say it was epilepsy; some say eye trouble; some say malarial fever, or insomnia, or migraine headaches. Others conjecture that Paul was a humpback. We do not know. But we do know that there was something that seemed to crush the life out of him. It was terrible and it was hard—this we do know.

We ought to stop doctoring the picture in the church. There are miseries in your life and mine—and in our world—and we ought to be able to look honestly at them. Paul didn't call his misery "a blessing in disguise." He didn't spray it with perfume so as to make it smell like a rose. He says: "A thorn was given to me in the flesh, a messenger from Satan, to harass me from being too elated!" A thorn pierces the flesh and hurts. It came from the "Devil" says Paul, not from God.

We ought to realize that there are marriages that are ragged at the seams, there are families into which children ought not to have been born, and there are sicknesses, wars, and oppressions as a result of racism and sexism. All of us have some thorns which could help to make hell out of our world, jungles out of our homes, and misery out of our lives. Listen to Paul: "Three times I besought the Lord about this, that is should leave me; but he said to me, 'My grace is sufficient for you, for my power is made perfect in weakness.' "

Paul continues by saying in effect: "That prayer was so long ago. And, you know, I've still got the problem, but I've learned to live with it—and all sorts of insults and persecutions and disappointments and calamities—for when I am weak, it is then that I become strong."

The record is clear, Paul's thorn remained but he discovered that he relied more heavily on the grace of God. The Lord's answer to his prayer was: "My grace is sufficient for you, for my power is made perfect in weakness." This grace was large enough to bear the thorn and to carry him. He would be able to go on his missionary journeys all over the known world. He would be inconvenienced and he would suffer, and often, he would ache. But he would continue to fight and in the end, he would win, for he would find God's grace sufficient for every need.

For Jesus in the garden of Gethsemane, there was no escaping the cross. For Paul there was no escaping the thorns and sufferings of his ministry. For you and me, we can expect our Christianity to get us into trouble; to provide the presence of God, and to provide grace not for escape, but for victory without pride.

PRIVILEGE AND CHALLENGE

CHARLES SHELBY ROOKS

President of Chicago Theological Seminary
Chicago, Illinois

For to you has been given the privilege . . . not only of trusting him but also of suffering for him.

—Philippians 1:29

One of the most remarkable persons I have ever known was a woman I knew less than a year. In 1953, fresh out of seminary, I went to Washington to be her pastor. She was then within twenty-three days of reaching her ninetieth birthday. The most vivid mental picture I retain about her is her sitting in the second pew each Sunday holding up her hearing aid to make certain she heard everything said! Completely unembarrassed by her partial deafness, she was vitally interested in everything around her.

Probably you have never heard of this woman, but her name was Mary Church Terrell. She was then the widow of the first black judge in the Municipal Court of the District of Columbia. She was an 1884 graduate of Oberlin College, the first black person admitted to membership in the American Association of University Women, the first President of the National Association of Colored Women, as it was then called, and was honored by the Republican Party at its national convention in 1932. Altogether, hers was a remarkable and distinguished life.

When Mrs. Terrell was eighty-six, she joined three other Washington citizens in a test of racial discrimination against blacks in restaurants and other public accommodations by going to a downtown cafeteria where the four persons were refused service. A law forbidding such discrimination in public places had been passed by Congress in 1872, and was augmented by other laws in 1873, but from 1901 to 1950 those laws were ignored. For fifty years Washington was the only national capital in the world outside of Africa with a social philosophy of segregation.

When those forgotten laws were rediscovered, Mrs. Terrell was determined that they should be tested and enforced. She organized and was President for a long-named committee, The Coordinating Committee for the Enforcement of the District of Columbia Anti-Discrimination Laws, and she put herself on the front lines of any possible abuse or maltreatment that might eventuate. Incidentally, the attorney of record for the committee was Margaret Heywood, the first black woman to be Moderator of the United Church of Christ. In June 1953, three years later, the Supreme Court ruled that the 1872-73 civil rights laws were indeed still valid, and Mrs. Terrell had helped secure a significant victory in American social life. At the public celebration of her ninetieth birthday that September she called it "the longest and hardest (campaign) of my career." Ten months later she was dead.

This is a sermon about triumph over suffering, and I tell you Mrs. Terrell's story for three reasons. First, we need to claim the privilege of being alive and being a Christian at every stage of life. In the ordinary course of things all of us find life difficult. We are often frustrated, discouraged, fearful, or just downright tired. Much of the mental and physical anguish that comes to us seems unjustified or without reason. Mary Church Terrell, for instance, could never find satisfactory legal, moral, religious, or even humane reasons for the suffering she endured because she was black; she could not purchase a meal where other citizens did or go to places other citizens could. Life is difficult and the suffering which is inevitable often fails to make sense.

It was that way for Paul's friends at Philippi. They couldn't understand why he was in prison. He was a Roman citizen, and entitled to the protection of the Empire. Why should he be in prison? Also, Jews in their city were beginning to persecute them because the new religion they professed was an offense to Jews and to

Romans as well. What would happen to them if the friends who had brought this new faith suddenly died in jail? Their world was beginning to crumble around them, and their uncertainties were growing, much the same as they sometimes do when you and I are visited by trouble.

One way human beings deal with the trials of life is to hold all their depth of personal feelings inside while wearing a mask that hides the truth of turmoil. Paul Lawrence Dunbar understood well the terror and suffering of being black in this society. He wrote:

> We wear the mask that grins and lies,
> It hides our cheeks and shades our eyes.
> This debt we pay to human guile;
> With torn and bleeding hearts we smile.
> And mouth and myriad subtleties.
>
> We smile, but, O great Christ, our cries
> To Thee from tortured souls arise.
> We sing, but oh the clay is vile
> Beneath our feet, and long the mile;
> But let the world dream otherwise,
> We wear the mask.

There beneath the smile of the black minstrel, his soul and the soul of a whole people weep and continue to weep. One reaction to suffering is to wear a mask above the face of truth.

But Paul suggests another, a better way! Those Philippians were finding life overwhelming. Christ was costing more than they had estimated. And Paul doesn't console them, he congratulates them. He doesn't pity them, he envies them. "You have been given the privilege," he tells them, "not only of trusting Jesus Christ, but also of suffering for him, of giving him the blood and sweat and tears of your life." That's something to be sought, and to find glory in. It's what makes each moment rich and vital and joyous. Why, even in prison, he tells them that living means new opportunities for Christ. That's what the good news of the gospel is all about. "To you has been given the privilege not only of trusting him, but even of suffering for him as well."

The Apostle neither denies nor minimizes the misery of suffering. Suffering is real for every life—sometime, somewhere. Its possibility awakes with every dawn. But Paul has found the joyous, vital secret of life: that only total immersion in a great cause gives meaning and significance to our days. That cause for Paul is to tell the marvelous story of Jesus Christ through word and deed. That's the privilege of being a Christian. The challenge is to use even life's sufferings for that purpose. He could have gotten out of prision at any time by invoking his rights of Roman citizenship. But he realized his impending trial would enable many more people to hear about Jesus. Whatever he had to endure, therefore, was useful to Christ. The challenge for his friends at Philippi was to use their own suffering for the sake of the gospel. It is that possibility and joy which makes life whole.

My friend, Mary Church Terrell, saw that truth too. She was willing to risk shame, and vile words, and even physical harm in old age because her knowledge of Christ had taught her something vital about human dignity and about justice for all the people of this earth. She told the story of Jesus in deed even more than in words. And she accepted with great joy the opportunity even to suffer for his sake. To you and to me also has been given the privilege not only of trusting him but also of suffering for him. That's the great secret of life!

Now in the second place note that both privilege and challenge never end. They are a constant mark of life.

In his letter to his friends at Philippi, Paul is ambivalent about the relative merits of life and death. On the one hand, death means the marvelous prospect of life forever with Christ; on the other hand, living means countless opportunities to tell others about him. Paul is torn about which is better. He seems to ask Hamlet's question, "To be or not to be, that is the question." He seems almost to long for death. But he concludes finally that so much remains to be done for Christ in this world that he has reason enough to live.

Not many of us are undecided about life in just that way. No matter whether life is terrifying or unsatisfying, we hold onto its breath desperately. There is within us a tremendously strong will to live that struggles against every assault of terror or tedium, of pain or panic, of fright or fear. You and I want to live—usually at all costs, in whatever circumstances—maybe because we know, as the old spiritual says, that "Everybody talkin' 'bout heaven ain't goin' there!"

There is a difference, however, in living and in just being alive. The truth is, being alive is only a basic human instinct. The struggle to live, however, calls for faith and courage at every stage of our existence. What I'm talking about, you see, is the difference between satisfaction with simply getting from one day to the next, and the quality and content of what happens with those days. It isn't enough merely to count the hours and the days as they roll by. The privilege and challenge of being a Christian is the opportunity to take these marvelous days that God has given us and use them for him and for his children in the world. That takes courage because it is so much easier to ride the waves of life than to resist them.

The most remarkable thing about Mary Church Terrell was her courage—a courage she retained to the last moment of life. It was a trait of her black forebears in this nation, their chief legacy to us. In slavery and segregation they were called upon daily to live with inventive courage. They discovered that courage in Jesus Christ. It put a song on their lips and a trust in their hearts. With it they were sure God would deliver them. Do you remember even the titles of the songs they sang, their message of faith in God's final mercy despite awful suffering?

> "Swing Low, Sweet Chariot"
> "I've Got to Walk This
>   Lonesome Valley"
> "I'm So Glad Trouble Don't Last
>   Always"
> "Steal Away to Jesus"
> "Ride On, King Jesus"
> "Deep River"
> "Every Time I Feel the Spirit"
> "Didn't My Lord Deliver Daniel"

Those simple titles afford us a bare glimpse of the marvelous story about a people who found the God of Jesus Christ on these shores, who passed along their profound understanding of trust and courage in the midst of suffering. In recent years some young black people have ridiculed that quality of life. They said it wasn't the right ammunition for the revolution in which we're engaged. Black folk have to get power, they say, and they are right about that. Power is needed. Only what kind of power? That's the key question. The Apostle Paul, Mary Church Terrell, Martin Luther King, Jr., and countless others through history discovered that real power begins *within.* It comes from faith in a God who has demonstrated his love for us in the past and in the present. It comes also from the courage Christ gives us to take any suffering the day brings and transform it into creative deeds and words for his sake. The power enables us to act and live instead of merely being alive. That is our privilege and challenge which never ends. It is the second greatest secret of life that awaits our discovery.

Now third, and finally, the privilege and challenge, to which Paul points us, brings joy, enthusiasm, and vitality to life. Someone has remarked that the word *joy* and its various equivalents is found more often in this short letter to the Philippians than in all of Paul's other letters put together. That's a strange thing considering the circumstances under which he wrote. He was in prison, and the experience wasn't an easy one. He faced a trial whose outcome was uncertain. He faced the possibility even of death. That's a strange time to use the word *joy* especially so often and effusively. But it is that very background which gives the word such great significance.

In the closing chapter of his letter Paul tells us: "Always be full of joy in the Lord; I say again, rejoice! If you do this, you will experience God's peace, which is far more wonderful than the human mind can understand." He is sure that through the sufferings he has lost all earthly comforts, but discovered the one happiness he can never lose. He tries to tell the Philippians that secret. They were complaining about their troubles, but he recalls their knowledge about the presence of Christ in their lives, about the promises Christ has made to them. Whatever happened, they could rejoice in Christ. In the inward joy they would find power to endure and power to overcome, a new vitality and enthusiasm for each day's need. It is a marvelous transformation of the very idea of suffering.

Paul repeats another word constantly in this letter also,

sometimes two or three times in the same verse. It is the word *all* or *always.* He has found new meaning here also. Since his conversion Paul had trusted Christ and worked for him in years of hope and activity. Even under his changed conditions, he is certain Christ is present, that the gospel is valid for all times and circumstances.

As he brings the letter to a close he sums up the meaning of all he has written: "My beloved friends, stay true to the Lord." Whatever their troubles or fears, they must hold to the truth as they have learned it, assured that they can stand fast in it amidst all changes. He calls on his readers to look beyond the conclusions of this hour to the final and ultimate issue. When they stand in the Lord's presence at last, this earthly life, with its pride and ambition, its troubles and apprehensions and sufferings, will seem as nothing. "Try to measure life by that," he says, "for that is what really matters."

I'm sure that for some of the Philippians, as well as for some of us, Paul's message is convincing. There is no proof in it acceptable to ancient or modern minds. How do we know that all this will happen? The answer is, we don't if we require rational or scientific proof. But Paul was certain that suffering for Christ brought joy. He was convinced that this joy never ended. And he looked forward with enthusiasm to the opportunities of each new day. I've seen all that happen in the lives of enough people I've known to believe it is the great truth of life. It's why I have remembered Mary Church Terrell for nearly a quarter century. I trust that. And I trust what God has done for me through all my years.

ON REMEMBERING WHO WE ARE

GARDNER C. TAYLOR

Minister of The Concord Baptist Church of Christ
New York, New York

And when he came to himself, he said, How many hired servants of
my father's have bread enough and to spare, and I perish with
hunger! I will arise and go to my father, and will say unto him, Father I
have sinned against heaven, and before thee.

—Luke 15:17-18

In Alex Haley's monumental book, *Roots,* there are many pathetic,
almost unbearably touching accounts. Few will be more gripping
than that which treats of Kunta Kinte's first face-to-face meeting
with somebody else who like himself has been brought but recently
from Africa as a slave.

Kunta, driving the slave-owning physician's carriage, went to a
neighboring plantation. Through the fall evening, he suddenly heard
someone playing music in the slave quarters. The style of the music
told Kunta Kinte that the musician was an African who had not yet
lost the pure ways and sounds of Africa.

At the first opportunity, Kunta seeks out the other African and
they engage in conversation. He discovers that the other African is
from Ghana as Kinte was from Gambia. They recall in the conversation many of the ways and sayings of their home far across the sea
which neither would likely ever see again.

When their evening together is passed and Kunta Kinte has
returned to his plantation and cabin, he reflects on what has happened to him. With the slave masters and other slaves—for different reasons perhaps—opposed to any signs of African ways and

language, Kunta Kinte realizes suddenly that his heritage, his identity, who he was in terms of the structures of family and place and language and religion and tribe, have all been taken away from him. "Day by day, year by year, he had become less resisting, more accepting, until finally, without even realizing it he had forgotten who he was."

"He had forgotten who he was." This sentence states the great crisis of identity. All people need to find who they are in terms of their particular place in history, the circumstances which have shaped their outlook and more or less determined their role in the society of which they are a part. Much that came out of the "black is beautiful" period was froth and foam, sound and fury, but then that is true of anything. One of the enduring and authentic pluses, no, one of the enduring and authentic indispensables which came out of that time was the discovery, or rediscovery, of something precious and splendid in the background of black people in America. All people need to sort out the pieces and put their hands and hearts on the greatness and on the promise which they possess because of what they have passed through. All people must wrestle with that, with remembering who they are.

Deeper than race or point of origin is the question which each human with a normal inquisitiveness must ask himself and herself: "Who am I?" The answers come at us thick and fast, and God help us if we settle for small incomplete answers!" "Who am I?" we ask. Science answers: "Protoplasm, cells, blood, bones, flesh," and adds "an incredibly and amazingly wonderful 'system of plumbing and pumping and locomotion.' " "Well and good," we say, but the question still persists, "Who am I?" "Mind and thought, dreams and impulses that lie below the level of awareness, in the cellars and dungeons of the unconscious," psychology says in explaining us humans as it sees us. We bow our heads in agreement, but the question still naggingly raises itself, "Who am I?" "A unit in some system of work and rewards, of economics, labor and money, that's what we are," says the materialist who sees all of life and history in terms of bread and butter. Yes, we recognize truth in all of these things, and others, but we are not satisfied. "Who am I?"—the question will not disappear. Common sense gives its clipped, terse answers: an American, a Baptist, a black (or a white), a Democrat (or a Republican), a laborer, a consumer, a patient, a retiree, and on and on. And yet the question haunts.

We have connections, spiritual ones if you please, which none of these categories explains, indeed, we have spiritual connections which all of these categories together do *not* explain. We turn to that amazing and life-affirming document which we call the New Testament and find some sharp rejoinders and rebukes to the explanations given to us by science and psychology and economics. To the claim that we are flesh and blood, the New Testament replies, "Flesh and blood cannot inherit the kingdom of God." Likewise, when we are told that we are mind and thought and impulses, the New Testament replies that our mind and all that it entails can be twisted and warped. One shudders on reading the words of Romans 1:28, "And even as they did not like to retain God in their knowledge, God gave them over to a reprobate mind." When we are told that we are economic beings we nod politely, and recognize that there is some truth in the assertion. At the same time we sense that something is missing in this definition of who we are. We are certain something is missing when we hear Jesus say, "Man shall not live by bread alone," and we have all of us known times when we had more than enough physical food, more than enough bread, and still felt very hungry, very empty, to the point of ache and pain.

We turn to Jesus for guidance as to who we are, for is he not our way and our truth and our life? Ah, Christian, here is a precious truth which you must never let slip from your firm grip and grasp. We are not stumbling in the dark as to how we shall act, what we should believe, upon what we should base the conduct of our lives. He is our standard; Christ is our guide. Oh, surely we must use our minds and feelings and imagination in finding his will for our lives. But we have the tape measure, the carpenter's square, the scales, the light meter, the sailor's compass, the spiritual calculator, Christ Jesus! And so we turn to him to find out who we are.

The fifteenth chapter of Luke deals with a family of two sons, both of whom in separate ways broke the heart of the father who loved them both dearly. George Murray called the parable "the most divinely tender and the most humanly touching story ever told on earth." It is a slice of the divine heartbreak. The centuries have indelibly labeled it "the parable of the prodigal son," though Edwin McNeil Poteat thought it should be called, "the parable of the prodigal father."

The parable tells of a home whose peace and quiet are broken by an insistent son who impudently asks his father for his part of the family inheritance, and that before the father's death. This, itself, was presumptuous and unfeeling. How heartless we can be sometimes! There lives on in my memory a bitter incident which happened in my ministry. A father came to me in the long ago and said that he wanted to deed the family house, his home, to the children while he still lived. I can understand that now, since the things of this world become increasingly unimportant and ever burdensome as we get along in years. I was young but something in me recoiled at the suggestion. Over my protests he did so. That man later returned to me with tears in his eyes and said that his children did not want him to use any part of the house except his one room.

"Give me," said the boy. Is this our perennial human heresy? Is this what is wrong with too many of us, too many of our children, our young people? "Give me." O surely, it pleases us that they ask, but where is the line between "give me" and "let me help?" I do not want them to go through what I had to go through, you say. But if what you went through helped put you in a position where you can help them, what is so wrong with them tasting a little of that?

And so the father gave the son what he asked and the boy left home. That leaving of home, under whatever circumstances, is one of the deeply touching scenes of family life. In this case the son went down. He lost what he had. He went from bad to worse. His clothes were thin and his sandals worn out. This young man's money was soon spent and his friends were soon gone. Unshaven, unkempt, down at the heels and desperate, he hired himself out and got a job feeding hogs. Think of it! Draw the comparison. A prince in a pigpen, an heir feeding hogs! Hungry, he almost stooped down to eat from the trough where the hogs ate.

Then said Jesus, "He came to himself." What is the Master saying? Is he not saying that this riotous spendthrift and bruiser of his father's heart is out of character? Do you catch the high compliment Jesus pays you and me even in our worst and most wayward moments? He is saying that when we are worst we are least ourselves. He is saying that in each of us there is what the old theologians called the *imago dei* ("image of God"). Overlaid we are with the rust of our willfulness and the dirt of our deeds and the slime and grime of our sinfulness, but underneath it all we are in the likeness of God.

We need to come to ourselves. Our nation desperately needs to see its mission in history as something more than greedy consumption. All of us need to see ourselves in terms of our true spiritual origins, in terms of some worthful purpose for our lives and in terms of our eternal destiny.

The air all around us is filled with voices telling us to come to ourselves. Weariness with the life we are living, meaninglessness, joylessness tell us "Come to yourself and live in God." The prizes for which we sell ourselves and which turn to dust in our hands remind us to find and to accept our true selves as "givers" rather than "getters." "Come to yourself." Sweeter voices also speak. Names and faces out of the dreary, dead past can remind us of better days and better selves. We read or hear of heroes and heroines whose stirring deeds and noble lives thrill us with an awareness of something august and god-like in us. The Savior's dying love calls, placing at Calvary the price tag he puts on our work and our destiny. Yes, there are stirrings in us. We have only to heed them and to recognize them for what they are, the proddings of God prompting us toward remembering who we really are—and whose!

WILT THOU BE MADE WHOLE?

DONALD R. WHEELOCK

President of Saints Academy
Lexington, Mississippi

When Jesus saw him lie, and knew that he had been now a long time in that case, he saith unto him, Wilt thou be made whole?

—John 5:6

The scene depicted in this text provides a classical model and a succinct representation of Jesus' entire mission and ministry, which sought to bring the restorative powers of God's grace to bear on the wide spectrum of the vexing problems of human existence. Here we find Jesus far removed from the elaborate parlors of the upper echelons of society's social hierarchy, and his distance from these sheltered provinces is strikingly underscored by the observation that he is surrounded by a "great multitude of impotent folk," the blind, crippled, paralyzed, and atrophied. The five-porch pool adjacent to the sheep market, Bethesda (House of Grace), had become a virtual charity hospital for those whose extremes of disability adamantly defied the powers of the sagacious medicine men. And thus these victims of irrevocable circumstance were left huddled together in somber anticipation of the moving of the pool's water—a signal that the water freshly impregnated with healing power, was applicable to the ills of him who first entered it.

Not only does Jesus come to the aid of this distressed throng of suffering humanity, he proceeds to its worst case, a man infirm for thirty-eight years, almost completely lacking in the necessary mobility to reach the water. At this point, an interesting brief scenario ensues. Jesus' healing of this ailing gentleman was prefaced by the question, "Wilt thou be made whole?" or in more current terminology, "Do you want to become well?" It would appear that Jesus could have healed this invalid by sheer fiat without regard for his essential disposition toward the imminent prospect of recovery by a means that Jesus would provide. Jesus' question implied and conveyed much more meaning and import than is apparent upon cursory perusal. The man's very presence at the pool could have been taken as sufficient indication that he desired to be well. However, Jesus, knowing that this was not sufficient, investigates the interiority of this man and seeks his response by direct confrontation with this soul-searching question.

When the Bethesda incident is projected onto the panoramic screen of the entirety of human existence, a clue is gained for the proper understanding of the role of the church in ministering to the larger world context. The gospel and the preaching thereof, both by precept and example, is essentially the creation of a confrontation-event in which humanity, collective and individual, is invited to explore the possibility of gaining the wholeness seemingly promised on every side but never quite delivered as an experienced reality. Humankind outside of the circle of faith observes these great pools of opportunity and even draws nigh thereunto only to find itself crippled in its capacity to bathe in these soothing waters of contemplated possibility.

While this is true of the broader scope of human existence, nowhere in America do we meet more dramatically with this phenomenon of "pool-side paralysis" than in the black community. In a most striking manner we meet the keen possibility of full positive self-actualization blunted and shackled, not only by the regularly encountered diseases that infect men's souls, but further by social circumstances designed and perpetuated to the end that blacks may heap material upon spiritual woes. While yet a great throng of life's impaired persons—blind, lame and withered—sit beside the pools of life's implied promise of undiminished good, the worst condition, the plight of the Bethesda invalid, is reserved for America's black man.

The ministry of the church, and particularly the black church, has been one of rescuing souls from the tempting suicide plunge into the depths of despair and hopelessness. It has offered neither a pacifying opiate nor an invitation to an obsequious compliance with the social and spiritual ethos of the environment. But rather, it seeks to elucidate the radical life-changing implications of the biblical text we read a moment ago. Being in the worst condition only makes us the most eminent candidate for God's loving care. But we have tarried and hesitated too long in replying to the pointed question that Jesus always poses to people inextricably caught up in life's dilemmas. He asks today, even to you who now stare from the pew, "Wilt thou be made whole?" Do you really want to be free of impairment and disability? Do you really want to experience the undiminished entirety of the good that life offers?

There is a glib and superficial Yes which easily mounts the lips of the person confronted with this question but its manifest origin outside of the heart, or the deepest will, renders it invalid and causes it to be translated into its diametrical opposite. This superficial Yes arises out of the basic instinctual movement toward self-preservation. It is a basic axiom of even pedestrian philosophy that all life that is governed by rational or semirational processes is marked by the adoption of behavior which attempts to minimize disability, injury, incompleteness, and imbalance. Since Jesus' question is not only concerned with the end of deliverance but also the means of salvation, the response cannot be an easy answer drawn from natural tendencies or instinctual dispositions. It must be made within the full context of a total acceptance both of the bright prospects of the ends and the special requisites of the means.

In these latter years of protest and confrontation, we as a black people appear to be subject to a sweeping embarrassment which has further complicated the process and exacerbated the typical human hesitancy in answering Jesus' question in an affirmative that boasts the depth and sincerity of faith. This embarrassment has given rise to that thin and glib Yes which our fellowmen do not hear and God ignores. In recent years we have been assailed by the radical black activists who sharply condemned our trek across the wilderness to an unseen "promised land" which Martin Luther King had glimpsed and toward which he patiently marched singing "We shall overcome." In stark contrast to King's counsel of love, patience, endurance, and restraint, the radicals advised confrontation, violence, and the immediate wrestling of freedom and power from the hands of the oppressor. In the same breath they criticized the black church as a prime obstacle to freedom and as a headquarters of counterproductivity which fed the black masses an otherworldly pabulum which has the insidious and finally fatal effect of rendering oppressed people incapable of adequately perceiving and responding to their oppression. In this approach, Jesus' question is caricaturized either as the mistaken mutterings of a confused madman or the triumphal rhetoric of a cosmic superman, assuring the total conquest of white oppression and opposition.

In the midst of this attempt to eternally exile the Jesus of traditional black religion we of the circle of faith feel keenly pressed to fashion something of a rudimentary or fragmentary expression of what the professional theologians call theodicy, that is, to adopt reasoned argument to vouchsafe our conviction of the validity of those superlatives which in our experience make God be God. How can we claim to serve a God who is characterized as the ultimate ground of love, goodness, justice, and mercy when all around us we find the stubbornly incessant presence of evil following the course of world events? How can we assert that our God is the Creator and Sustainer of the world when ghetto existence shows the world to be so unlike our description of its Creator? Far be it from me to suggest that these penetrating questions are but perverse artifacts of the demonically possessed mind of the infidel. They well deserve our thoughtful consideration and reasoned reply. However, we must know the limits of our response possibilities.

Thoughtful representatives of the faith have considered this issue over the centuries and provide us with the standard arguments. Some have postulated the degrees of being and perfection and concluded that in this continuum, evil simply is nonbeing, the absence of good. Some envisioned two ultimate principles of reality (light/darkness, good/evil, God/Satan) and explained that the evil of the world is the result of an incomplete process in which God himself is overcoming the disorder of the universe. Yet some have pictured the despotic God whose sovereignty is identical with his righteousness. What he decrees from eternity is automatically right, and thus there is no such thing as evil. Others have maintained that God's power is limited by his own character of righteousness, truth, and love. Evil must be tolerated as a byproduct of the freedom that God grants to his creation. All of these conceptual offerings have their apparent merit but what we must fully appreciate is that no reasoned statement can be finally convincing to him who stands outside of the circle of faith. Rational explanation only provides a fleeting glimpse of an image seen through a glass darkly.

It is only through the gracious revelation of God in Christ, confirmed in our own experience, that we can truly come to "know" the good God that redeems our world even as it is. It is in the dawning of this context that humanity can hear as meaningful the question of the Master "Wilt thou be made whole?" and at the same time know that this is not vain interrogation but the sincere imploring of the One that promises to provide the wholeness and deliverance characterizing the good life. We have no need for embarrassment and neither do we have a need to picture Christ as our exclusive warrior who will crush white people and cause blackness to reign supreme. All have sinned, black, white, Jew, Gentile, and all are earnestly summoned to reply to the query, "Wilt thou be made whole?"

Yes, pool-side paralysis is everywhere to be seen—on our streets, in our schools and our homes—but just know that Jesus makes every Bethesda truly translate to "House of Grace." However, we must be as honest as the invalid who answered, "I have no one to put me into the pool." His was plea for help and ours must be the same. Jesus is ready when we accept the fact that truly he is the way, the truth, and the life. His model, sacrifice, and love have the capacity to remove us from a supine posture of the pool-side and place us in the mainstream of God's grace. When we admit that we need assistance in getting in the pool, the first significant step is taken on the road to salvation.

The ministry of the church ecumenical and even in the black community is dedicated and conducted to the end that man be brought to honestly confront the evil of his own sin and to the realization that he needs to be saved not only from the dread consequences of his sin but also from self-designed cures for felt ills. Our culture inculcates the notion of man's self sufficiency, and recent technological strides under the auspices of the religion of scientific methodology have supported the notion and strengthened the barriers to the acceptance of the implications of finitude. If one is not carried away by the sheer magnitude of the tide of indifferent secularism, there is still the plentitude of deceptive philosophies which purport to provide the answers to all problems.

We must know and continue to offer the truth that Andraé Crouch captured in song, "Jesus Is the Answer." As a Bethesda, Jesus both asks the question and provides the answer. The answer that he provides is not a speculative discourse on time and eternity. Surprisingly, the answer that he offers is himself, "hung up for our hang-ups" (Mattie Clark). The decision is yours and the time is now. "Wilt thou be made whole?"